FIND YOURSELF: A GUIDE TO SELF-AWARENESS

ISBN: 10: 0963551124
ISBN-13: 978-0963551122 (3J Press

DEDICATION

I would like to dedicate this book to my three sons. They have sacrificed and supported me while I wrote this book. They have encouraged me when I needed it the most. I would also like to dedicate this book to the hundreds of thousands of clients I encountered in my health care occupation. I learned a lot while giving them direct care and learned from their experiences.

INTRODUCTION

There are so many people writing so many books that promise to solve all our problems, cure all our ills. This isn't one of them. Shirley Rose Jones puts us to work.

This book advocates self-assessment, and the author gives us the benefit of experience. These are not words meant to provide easy solutions. Readers are advised to look around themselves and to look within. And that can be the hard part.

Believe if you want to that 'life is a little ship upon the sea; you can be happy if you let yourself be'. That's a passive approach. Jones sees each seeker after happiness as an individual who must do her or his own evaluation and then his or her own work. "The only one that you can compete with is yourself." You walk your own path by yourself. You are responsible for your own well-being. It's up to you to "fix your self- esteem," to "give yourself love."

Positive spirituality is combined with Christian faith in this book. The glowing force of the discussion on love is especially powerful, and it transcends sectarian bounds. Jones says, "We need love, and we need to give love." We must learn this lesson. We need exercises here as we have them for other chapters, but the sense of connection is not to be denied. Maybe this is the lesson of the whole work; maybe this is the work of this book.

The spiritual and the practical are nicely combined. The chapters on relationships are informative and show caring application of the author's health care training and experience. Jones says, most women don't mind men who have problems, but they resent men who don't have solutions or don't know how to seek solutions to their problems.

This is a how-to book that promotes honest analysis of both inner and outer self. It has been a joy to work with this author and to witness the dedication that she brings to her work. She practices what she preaches, and she preaches with passionate conviction. Be good to yourself. Read this book for yourself. Take these steps, make these choices, use these keys for yourself, to FIND YOURSELF. Dr. Rhoda Miller Martin was a professor of English at Spelman College.

Rhoda Miller Martin

ii

WHY I WROTE THIS BOOK

I have always been curious about how successful people achieved and carried out their dreams. Most importantly I am interested in why normal people never discovered their talent and never fulfilled their dreams. Many people know that they are here on earth to do something important but they spend a lifetime being unable to figure out what to do, how to do it and when to branch out into self-discovery. Being busy has taken over the average person's lives and we are in a web of having no personal development. The cycle of detachment from us and our personal need is catastrophic and before we leave this earth we owe it to ourselves to find ourselves and our position in life. This is a personal goal that we can reach but few of us do the necessary introspection and daily work to attain it.

In my over 30 years in health care I have talked to many people who live with the pain of having a dying dream within themselves. Their bodies are overcome with diseases and they are in a psychological state of sadness. They are in this frame of mind because they did not reach inside themselves to find the courage to achieve their goals in life. Destiny disappointment is a serious emotional pain that can also contribute to disease and discontentment in life. Many people who have major diseases have not considered the impact that this emotional void has on their health. They know this pain is there but they need support in confronting themselves and reaching in-ward to heal themselves from an unfulfilled destiny. They need encouragement in coming forth as a new discovered person.

The people around us are comfortable with whom they know us to be and may find it difficult to accept that we want to realize our true power. They may not understand that we want release from the load of whom people think us to be and we want to remove the blockage that hinder our personal growth. I feel that preparing a guide as this help to awaken people and aid them with tools to be gutsy in working on their self-development. These lessons are not given in schools. They are not learned at work as on-the-job training. Sometimes family circumstances do not promote the desperate need to give ourselves the attention necessary for our self-empowerment. Instead family dynamics can provide the environment for us to ignore these needs.

People want support to come to the realization that they have the ability to make positive change in their lives. They need this aid to empower themselves for personal growth that can begin now. They can read this guide and equip themselves with tools of self-discovery. People all over this world are so talented and if we find our true selves the world would be a better place for all of us to live in. When this work in us begins it brings joy and when it is completed it is productive for us and the nation. It is the happiness that we need to feel complete and to feel like we are a full part of the society we live in.

Many people commit to the grueling lifestyle of their full-time job for a lifetime. The problem is if they ignore the natural God-given talent within them which satisfy their personal destiny. Although many people are content with their jobs and are making a good salary they are not living a happy life. Their lives are crowded with stress, lack of finances, unhappiness, the inability to figure out how to get to the next level, being stagnated, meeting the needs of others and neglecting their own needs, and being self-defeated. The list is endless and is different for each of us according to our various circumstances. Our routine has become natural to us and seems impossible to change. This book provides the opportunity for each person to stop unhappiness and offer a pathway for a balanced and happy life. Each person has the capacity to put their lives on the path of wholeness and a rewarded destiny.

Some of us are stuck in a job that displeases us while we have natural entrepreneurship abilities that we are not pursuing. Instead we are being miserable working for someone and have not searched for the creativity within us. Our time is spent doing work we do not want to do and we do not spend any time finding out and doing what we love to do. We are not connected to the creativity that we have so we can conquer this internal conflict. We can do so much better in our lives when we figure out exactly what is it we should do to change our situations. This book is a journey that helps us peel off layers of being immerge in the worldwide trap of not knowing our true selves. This book encourages us not to be lost or confused in our daily living. It helps us become the person who emerges with a defined purpose in life and is using every day to perform our purpose.

WHY YOU SHOULD READ THIS BOOK

You should read this book to discover the secrets of having super self-confidence. This book shows you how to have a highly innovative life and how to solve problems with ease. In this book you will see how to attain enormous success in life. Whoever wants happiness, health, peace, wealth...and much more it's all here in this book. The time for re-evaluation of your life is NOW. Don't miss this chance to ask yourself if you achieved what you had hoped, did you get off tract, or do you feel emotionally paralyzed?

Is your wish-list or the goals berried in your soul activated? Don't feel alone because you can boost your motivation and turn the keys within YOU towards the right direction. All of your life's baggage can be dropped today when you stop! Then redirect yourself to a self-esteem boost in this book. Your life can have real meaning everyday with personal growth and self-improvement. There is no need to feel like you are in the dark staggering your way through difficulties, instead grab this movement of self-esteem activities, self-awareness plan, esteem quizzes and more...Get involve TODAY in building a life's plan from the top of your wish-list down to the bottom of it. However, start living what's on your wish-list from the bottom up to the top. If you have ever lost anything in life like faith, dignity, wealth, good health, trust, confidence or other personal attributes now is the time to repossess them.

There are guidelines shared here to show you how to take them back. Find Yourself: A Guide to Self-Awareness teaches you how to turn challenges into opportunities. At the core of this guide is a favorable time to exchange mental tiredness for bursting energy of new perspective, mental awakening and ascertain keys to ignite your success. In this guide losing at the only life you have to live is not an option. As an alternative many keys are given to shift you in the path of positive change and achievement. It is the book that is fully loaded with powerful life tools to lively you up and bring you the joy and happiness in life that we crave to own.

This book show you how to get the edge that make you stands out in a crowd. You learn to be more than just smart; you learn to be inspiring! It discuss how to use the deepest thinking part of you, to get whatever you want out of life . . . money, personal influence, love, respect and admiration. By unlocking this power and creativity your mind is ready to automatically improve your memory, and strengthen other mental powers to cast out self-doubt and self-defeat. Find Yourself: A Guide To Self-Awareness teaches powerful life tools, confidence, courage and bring out latent talents. It shows you that you can **grow rich** ... <u>in all things</u> ... material as well as spiritual. Join thousands of people across America who used this step-by-step guide to achieve success!

CONTENTS

ACKNOWLEDGMENTS

It is because of the gift and the creativity that God has given me that I am able to share this knowledge in this book. I give praises to God for all of His blessings and for giving me the strength and the endurance to write another book. There is no other brother like my oldest brother, Alvin, who has truly been there for me. Thanks to my sister Lavon, my brothers Wayne and Rivington.

I thank Dr. Rhoda Miller Martin, who did the first and the second editing on this book. You are an inspiration and a great teacher. You have encouraged me to take my writing to a more meaningful level. Heartfelt thanks to Marcia Stokes a friend and prayer worrier. Vince Gillam, thanks for creating the book cover. You are a friend and the greatest artist I have known.

1 FINDING HAPPINESS

Happiness is an emotion that everyone must achieve and enjoy. We should know that even an unhappy person can learn to become happy and that happiness can be practiced by all of us. Many of us make the mistake of thinking that finding happiness is complicated and that having happiness is hard to achieve. We demonstrate this belief by thinking that happiness is a feeling that must be motivated by a lover, a spouse, or a friend. Also, we demonstrate this thinking when so many of us become dependent on others such as boyfriends, girlfriends, or pleasant situations to make us happy. In this case, when the lover, spouse, friend and pleasant situations are not available, we easily fall into the mode of unhappiness.

We should realize that happiness based on personal relationships only, is temporary and is unstable. Permanent happiness comes from within you and not from others or from comforting situations. If we have not learned how to make ourselves happy, then no one can make us happy. So let the search begin within us so that we can find out what we can do to discover our happiness. We must become quite clear about what happiness really means.

Although happiness is understood as a feeling of joy and pleasure in varying degrees, it is necessary not to categorize happiness as just having fun. In many ways, happiness and fun are two different emotions. While fun is momentary and ends when the action that caused the amusement ends, happiness is unceasing. Happiness is a continued state of feeling good about yourself, your life, and your environment. Happiness also includes a state of lasting internal and external pleasure and fulfillment.

At this point let us distinguish between fun and happiness even more by relating them to our teenage years. Many of us can remember that parts of our teenage years might have been fun but other parts were often very unhappy. We can remember that our desire to have fun caused us to do many unfortunate things during these years. During our teenage years we did not understand that fun was temporary and that it was happiness that we really needed. Due to this reason many of us should be able to relate to the many teens of today who have gone astray or who have happiness confused with fun. Also, many teens have taken the wrong turn in life.

We can now understand that many mistakes are made due to unhappiness or because many teenagers confuse happiness with fun. Also, although many of our teenage years could be termed as lots of fun, we can also recall that these highs were short-term and temporary. These so-called fun times were uncertain and often unhappy. For example, some of us can recall reaching for pleasure by doing ugly pranks or by degrading someone and hurting their feelings, just for a momentary cheap laugh. We now know that behaviors like this certainly do not bring happiness.

However, we must understand that some of the things that we have done as a teenager or during weak moments indicate that we needed happiness. It is imperative that we also distinguish between fun and happiness in order to move on to permanent happiness. Taking this step is necessary for all of us. In this distinguishing we cannot confuse our teenage years with happy times and continue to live as teenagers in our adult life. We should make the transition and change the perception of our minds. Begin by doing good deeds both for other people and for yourself. Doing good deeds will leave a permanent imprint or reference on other people's hearts and on your own heart. These actions are demonstrative of happiness being distributed.

Initiate happiness by distributing it and by enjoying the partaking in its distribution. This gives you some positive characteristics about yourself that you can cultivate. This also makes you look and feel better about yourself and improves self-awareness. Developing awareness of your good characteristics and yourself enhances happiness. This happiness is also enhanced when you understand your experiences and when you become comfortable with your own past, present, and future in this world. Happiness is enhanced when you become pleased with your own disposition and when you keep your focus on the 'real' things in your life.

During your lifetime, you must learn the 'real' things in your life. Some of the 'real' things that you must focus on are developing your faith and establishing your happiness. You must focus on improving yourself and discover knowledge about the destiny that you must fulfill. You must focus daily on the love that you give to yourself and to others. You must focus on your small and your large accomplishments and make them meaningful by enjoying them. Finally, you must focus on finding a balance in your life. In order to be happy, you must put importance on balancing all of your emotions and all of your situations.

You must also be aware of those things that are not the 'real' things in your life. Take notice that a lot of money, expensive possessions or some good or bad personal relationships are not the 'real' things in your life and they do not make a person happy. In order to be happy you must feel pleasant and be content with yourself, despite the lack of or the abundance of money, substance, or friends. Many rich people remain very unhappy because they are not pleased or content with all areas of their own lives. Therefore, such substance is not essential for happiness.

On the other hand, many people who are momentarily poor but who have made a concentrated effort to strengthen the weaknesses in their own lives are very comfortable with themselves and are very happy. Fortunately for us, we are not born prima donnas or perfect, but we are given the power, the knowledge, the wisdom, the ability, and the resources to develop that which we lack. Therefore, happiness comes from within and is eminent when an individual has taken every opportunity to grow and to strengthen their weaknesses. Also, when an individual is successfully working on his or her happiness the individual continues to cultivate him or herself, thereby redefining their characteristics every waking moment. This does not mean that self should consume the individual but it means that he or she should be hands-on and in charge of working on his or her happiness. When a person likes what he or she has become and the outer reflection of what he or she can see inside of themselves, then he or she is on their way to happiness.

A person should never allow any outside force to manipulate the happiness that they have obtained. Many professionals as well as nonprofessionals have allowed their jobs and their careers to control their happiness. Instead of allowing their job, their salary, and their job status to cause them unhappiness, they can effect or change these unhappy situations. Since many of us spend a great deal of time at work, we must make the job fulfilling and rewarding. We must make our happiness impact upon our jobs to change our job situations. A happy person will find a way to do something creative to stabilize the unhappiness that a job or dissatisfying career can bring. Also, a person's desire for happiness will force them out of an unhappy career and not allow them to settle for unhappiness. At all times, happiness is strong and powerful enough to destroy the yokes of unhappy circumstances or the yokes of an unhappy environment.

In order to ensure and to protect our happiness, we should be certain that our job repays us in many ways. For example, as we invest ourselves in our jobs, we should be certain that we receive respect, support, and at least a moderate amount of pleasure from our daily job. We should make certain that our jobs are fulfilling and pleasurable to us. On the other hand, if we do not enjoy our jobs while constantly investing ourselves into work, if we do not get anything in return, then we will definitely feel out of control and unhappy. We will feel unpleasantness and a sense of un-centeredness. If this happens, demand control!

There should always be that fair exchange between work and fulfillment. If we are unfulfilled by our job we need to find a job that fulfills us or we need to change the job situation to make it fulfilling. It may take years to reach this level, but the effort and the attempt to change the unhappy circumstances should be in process. In some cases, some of us are unhappy because we are displeased with our position in life or because our family circumstances may be difficult. Despite these well-founded reasons, we still have the choice to take control over any unpleasant situation and to become happier people.

Whenever a person is unhappy in one area of their lives, this unhappiness affects other areas of their lives. Also, if a person is unhappy about a particular situation on their job, depending on a romantic relationship for happiness cannot rectify the unhappiness. Such unhappiness requires that the person take action and do something to change the unhappy circumstances. Start by examining yourself and getting to know more about yourself. 'Know yourself' is a philosophy that you must embark upon in order to take action and to help change unhappy circumstances.

To know yourself means assessing your life and acknowledging the areas in your life that make you happy and those areas that make you unhappy. After these facts are known, then you must go to work to do that which is necessary to change the distinct areas of displeasure or unhappiness in your own life. From year to year you should discover something about yourself that you can improve, and you should become happier when you improve these areas. Happiness is a growing phenomenon, while standing still can be devastating to an individual when there are no improvements. When your happiness is neglected, it may result in depression. Therefore, we need lessons so that we may be equipped to establish and to maintain our happiness.

The lessons on how to become a happy person are not taught in schools. It is incumbent upon everyone to find happiness himself or herself. In many cases, society just doesn't care about this personal need. Society is more concerned about production and performance. For these reasons we must care about our own happiness by getting to know our strengths and our weakness instead of just producing and performing every day. We must know our strengths and weaknesses but we must not measure ourselves by someone else's strengths and weaknesses; we should not compete with others. If we measure ourselves by someone else's strengths and weaknesses we can become frustrated and confused. When we measure ourselves by someone else's strengths and weaknesses we set ourselves up to have jealousy towards the person that we are competing against. Instead, reverse it and dwell on your strength. Learn from reading a book or from observing others who are good in your weak areas instead of competing or becoming jealous. Learn how to strengthen your weaknesses.

Happiness is more prominent when we are doing something about our weaknesses or unhappy situations. Competing with friends is not beneficial. Therefore, become comfortable and accept the mistakes, the decisions, and the challenges that are in your own life. Now the only one that you can compete with is yourself, by measuring the level of growth and improvement that you make every day. What your friends are doing or what your friends have accomplished is good for those friends and is an encouragement to everyone. However, try concentrating in a positive manner on the terrific job that they have done for themselves and ask how you might use it. Learning from others can improve your happiness and help you to change your life.

One of my testimonies is that when I reflect on my life, I can look at myself and be thankful for the great work God has done in my life. I am glad for what my mother has done in my life. I can be eternally grateful to my friends for being a wonderful part of my life. Most importantly, I am most happy with the fact that I listen, I read, and I agree to do a terrific job with my own life, and this growth continues. If everyone felt this good and terrific about their own lives, then internally they would meet the definition of being a happy person.

Happiness must be sincere and must be separated from negative emotions such as guilt, shame, and family secrets. Guilt is a quiet emotion that must be pulled forward and deleted because it invades on happiness. We must search our family history, our past, and ourselves. We must be sure that we are not carrying family secrets or what we see as family shame. A history of family secrets and shame weighs us down and ties us up in unhappiness. In this case, we must go through the steps that are necessary to resolve these family issues. We can only be happy when we are free from such issues and can honestly say that the problem is resolved --- and mean it.

Guilt is certainly one of the heavy weights that interfere with happiness. Therefore, whatever it is that we may be guilty about we must confront, resolve, and then dismiss all guilt. Be true to yourself and expose your guilt in the right way, to the right person, and in the right setting; then let go of all shame and guilt in this process of preventing despondency. Unhappiness and guilt stunt this process called growth and development, and we must overcome them to become happy individuals and to live in peace.

Finding peace with yourself is included in the sphere of happiness. Peace, being alone, and happiness are all related at some point. Some of us may know someone who just cannot tolerate being alone and we often can relate to his or her feelings. We call these feelings loneliness. We relate, and yet it is difficult to understand what could be so bad about being alone. But still some of us just couldn't stand the way that being lonely made us feel. As complex as this question may seem, it still must be answered. Is a person so unhappy with himself or herself that he or she hates spending time alone? And if this is the case, that a person makes himself or herself miserable, how then could someone else like being around that person?

Only when a person can utilize and enjoy their time alone are they able to enjoy the essence of a relationship without demanding that their spouse or friends constantly be around them. When this happens a person can feel the climax of a relationship; they are not relying on another imperfect person to keep them feeling good about themselves and about life. When this happens, they already feel good about themselves, their life, and are able to use their positives to balance their negatives. This loneliness, or what I call quiet time, is a time that can be used to reflect on and to enjoy the great things that you can and will do in your own daily life. It is a time of peace and serenity. Happiness comes from a peace within the resources of your thinking, perceptions, and positive actions. These resources can bring comfort, which results in contentment and happiness.

We have the power, and the knowledge is available for us to develop into happy people despite our negative environment. We even have the power to change our environment over time. We have no reason to be locked into unhappiness or to put the impossible burden on someone else to make us happy. If there is an unhappy person around us who insists on making everyone else unhappy, then we have the power of defense. Many utilize the power of defense by communicating, ignoring, avoiding, and fighting back. Your happiness is worth defending. Communicating in this sense simply means speaking up for yourself when you are right and shielding your happiness. It means do not let an unhappy person impose their unhappiness on you.

Let them know that you will not tolerate their unhappy projection, and hold to your opinion. At times it may be necessary to ignore or to avoid unhappy people who want to remain unhappy. Don't feel guilty if you have to politely exit out of a conversation if it is imposing on your peace and your standards for happiness. If you put yourself in the position to be a victim of someone's unhappiness, you will always be a target for someone else's unhappiness. Be ready to protect the happy person that you have worked so hard to become.

Mood Changing Activities: Here Is A Beautiful Cycle Of Life Pleasures

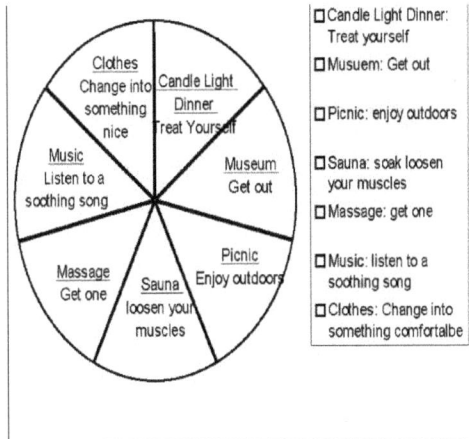

Put A Check Beside The Small Square Boxes Identifying The Activities That You Like The Most. Practice The Ones That You Like Several Times A Week.

Relaxation Activities

☐ Leisure time: Do nothing

☐ Read: Get a good book

☐ Write: Think of a poem

☐ Bath: The way you like it

☐ Sleep: Get enough rest

☐ Vacation: Every 6 months

Vacation Every 6 months

Lleisure time Do nothing

Sleep Get enough Rest

Read Get a good book

Bath The way you like it

Write Think of a poem

Check The Small Square Boxes That You Like Most And Practice Them Very Often. Extend This List By Adding Your Own Relaxing Activities. Put Your Activities In A Beautiful Circle

New Activities

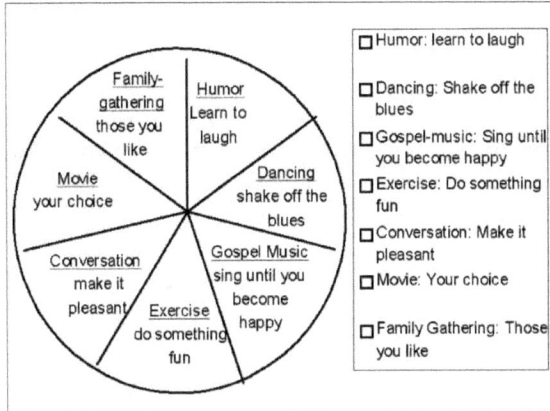

Humor: learn to laugh

Dancing: Shake off the blues

Gospel-music: Sing until you become happy

Exercise: Do something fun

Conversation: Make it pleasant

Movie: Your choice

Family Gathering: Those you like

Change Activities To Avoid A Routine, Avoid Predictability, And Avoid Boredom. You May Change As Often As Desired.

List three things that you can do with a friend to create a happy mood.

1.

2.

3.

List four things that are powerful and enjoyable enough to change your mood. You may include hobbies.

1.

2.

3.

4.

List three people with whom you can enjoy yourself at any given time.

1.

2.

3.

Put Your Notes To Yourself Here

2 VANQUISH YOUR FEARS

It was January 5, 1975, on a cold winter day. Snow had covered the ground for two weeks in New York City. The communities were shut down because all stores, federal buildings, and schools were closed. Snow piled up on the ground to a height of fifteen feet. Everyone was snug in their homes. It was a wonderful time to relax and to catch up on other things. Jack McDoodles was closed in at the penthouse with his girlfriend of ten years. She was wooed by him and was given everything that any woman could ask for--except marriage. For the duration of the relationship she tried to calm his fears and she tried to make him feel very secure while she hoped for the big day when he would propose marriage to her. After the twelfth year of their relationship, Melica realized that the big day wouldn't happen for her. She had to give up her wonderful man because his phobia of marriage conquered him. He allowed his fear to control his life, and he did nothing to conquer such a great fear. So he lost her.

The New Webster's dictionary defines fear as an instinctive emotion aroused by impending or seeming danger, pain, or evil. We must be aware and recognize what happens to this instinctive emotion in order to understand and eliminate fear. This instinctive emotion becomes a complex pattern of reactions that are aroused subconsciously. It therefore becomes an automatic reaction instead of a thought out action. Fear has existed for as long as man and has inhibited mankind throughout his lifetime. Remember, in the Garden of Eden Adam and Eve hid from God because of their fears.

Since fear is an instinctual emotion, we must force ourselves to trace our patterns of reactions. In other words, we must examine our fears by asking questions such as 'Why do I react this way?' 'Do I feel secure or insecure when certain situations happen?' Most of our fears stem from our formulated concepts of what we think of as the unknown. However, the only unknown is death. The truth is that every human being is faced with something that someone has already been through. Therefore, what we consider the unknown is well known to many, and such knowledge is imparted in a variety of books and through spiritual and motivational advice. Also, some of our fears have developed from past bad experience that caused physical, emotional, or psychological pain, and we are unwilling to go through or to feel those familiar pains again. It is a fact that pain and mankind do not agree. Other fears stem from not wanting to feel unfamiliar emotional pain, anticipated spiritual or physical pain and other hardships. But "no pain, no gain."

Let's begin to acknowledge our fears, which is the initial process of overcoming them. All of mankind must first accept the philosophy that life is painful, and no matter what we do none of us can go through life without feeling some degree of pain. Some of us will endure greater pain than others, but we all will experience pain if we live long enough. Fear cannot stop this pain. There will be pain, fear, and suffering. Generally speaking, the growing pains of life do not do severe damage if the person experiencing them has healing methods to deal with this pain.

Deal with pain by accepting the fact that you are hurt. Treat spiritual, emotional, and psychological pain as you would treat physical pain. Do this by first giving the pain time to heal. For instance, if you just had surgery you would be in a lot of physical pain. You would need special care and time to heal. Therefore, use caution, gentleness, tenderness, comfort, love, and warmth very often, just as you would if you were in physical pain. Give these treatments to yourself and surround yourself with people who can supply these treatments to you. Don't allow the pain to be trapped inside of you by holding it secretly, but share it with someone in whom you have great confidence and who can help to assess the reasons for your hurt.

Hiding, covering, and protecting the source of pain will bury the pain deeper, but therapeutic exposure of secrets and secret pains can peel off ugly layers and lead to great freedom. Exposing secrets and secret pain releases you from shame and self-blame. If not released these secrets only lead to insecurity, which leads to fear. Such exposure results in you putting down the shame, putting the blame in its place and picking up self-esteem. Now, instead of fearing pain, use the conscious mind and not the instinctual emotions to properly manage pain. Take the time to cry and talk about it; empty out and then heal yourself. Let go of the baggage and fix your self-esteem.

Some great self-esteem builders are listening to motivational tapes, reading self-help books (such as this one), pampering and giving yourself a relaxation period every day. Other methods include removing all of the negativisms that are in your life one by one, talking to positive and encouraging people, and practicing hobbies that you enjoy. Also, pay yourself --- exercise regularly, eat a healthy diet, and don't allow anyone to control you. Use your power to keep your life stable and balanced. Learn from your bad experiences and use them to teach others, but never take such experiences personally. Confront pain, deal with pain honestly, and since there is healing for pain--you don't have to fear pain.

When fear tries to creep up on you because you lack knowledge about a particular area of life, use the conscious mind instead of the instinctual emotions. Remember that someone has successfully gone this route before; therefore it is not impossible to triumph in your circumstances. Reach out and take advantage of libraries and other resources such as friends, teachers, leaders, agencies, and heads of departments that are in your area. Read as much as you can and become familiar with information guides. The more resources you have and the more confident you can be in utilizing these resources, the less likely it is that you will be consumed with fear. Knowledge can help you to overcome many obstacles.

We can never store all of the information that we read or that we desire to remember in our brains. We can be equipped and ready to dig into available sources when necessary and obtain any information that we may need. There is an abundance of resources available. Therefore, there is no reason for anyone to be stuck in fear due to lack of knowledge. There is no reason to fear the unknown because death is the only unknown--and the Almighty is in charge of death. So don't let fear creep up on you. If anyone wants to be successful they must knock down their fears, because success is simply overcoming fears. When there are no fears, there are no limits.

Most people use the words 'timid' and 'shy' as a reason for lesser fears. However, they both stem from the same emotions, and they result in defeat. They break the will power that gives us the urgency to try again. Shyness and timidity do not benefit anyone; they limit us from reaching our ultimate goals and potentials. Shyness and timidity are the result of secret fears and will stop perseverance when there is the need to confront someone or something. From a practical point of view, not everyone is born bold and courageous, but everyone can become as bold and as courageous as they want to become. While some nervousness is normal, shyness can be replaced by boldness.

Shyness could be the result of a lack of confidence. This situation could lead to you being too concerned about other people's opinions and remarks. Shy persons should get to like and know themselves extremely well. There is a great possibility that if a shy person gives himself or herself love, they wouldn't be so concerned about the opinions and the remarks of others. One exercise that a shy person might want to do is to watch themselves and their mannerisms in the mirror. I believe that chances are they may just begin to love what they see about themselves.

A shy person should practice accentuating their positive characteristics. They must realize that as long as they are not disrespectful to anyone, the opinions of others are not as valuable as their own opinion about themselves. A shy person may want to use facts and scientifically proven resources to touch up the minor flaws that they feel they were born with, or they may choose to just accept these minor flaws. For example, if you are shy because of your speech, then use a tape and practice speaking. Listen to yourself, and appreciate yourself. Select those few characteristics that you feel ashamed of or shy about, and improve them or just accept them; then step out of that shyness. Practice expressing your feelings and speaking up for yourself.

You may even use the mirror to observe the faces and the various facial expressions that you like about yourself. Get a serious face, a funny face, etc. so that you will know and feel comfortable about how you look. However, don't become preoccupied with these activities, but get to know you well and validate yourself. After you have validated yourself, you don't need anyone else to approve of you. Be selective; search and get to know positive people and learn some up-lifting positive tips from them. Try to surround yourself with a variety of acquaintances and friends. Know that you are special no matter what others may say. Realize that situations which you have no control over will happen, but don't allow any situation to make you feel ashamed or make you crawl into a shell and become shy.

The fear of failure is one of the most common fears. Humans have the tendency to want to be able to defeat everything and every circumstance the first time around. How impossible! And where do we get the idea that we would be born into this world knowing how to conquer? Success is a lesson well learned, and most of the time it comes when we have learned how to operate the principles of life and the principles of the Bible. One of these principles reminds us that we have only failed when we fail to try one, two, and even three times, and sometimes even three times is not enough. Also, it is the experience that we gain from trying that is of most importance. These teaching experiences help us to grow and enhance our knowledge, whether we have so-called failed or not. Therefore, how can anyone call new experience failure? Also, from these new experiences we have acquired enough knowledge to make new efforts, including those efforts that will require a second or third attempt. Cancel the fear of failure by being open-minded, and look at a new project as if you are going to learn a lot, enjoy it, and grow from it. Do not dwell on whether or not you can do it, or if you have to do it over again.

For instance, when babies begin to walk they are not overcome by a fall. Although they fall numerous times, these falls do not mean that they have failed at walking. Bear in mind that everyone has tried something over and over again in his or her lifetime; you won't be the first or the last to tackle a task more than once. It might have taken many tries, but the points worth emphasizing are the achievements and the experiences; these overshadow any second or other attempts. However many tries it takes, you are still learning.

Fears can be as big as a giant or as small as a pin's head, but they often result in paralysis or stunted growth. The bigger the fear, the more stunted the growth. However, the only fear that is justified is the fear of danger. Other fears need to be handled. Fear is torment, confusion, and it clouds precise and accurate judgment. Fear is such a strong emotion that it can control other emotions if it is not dealt with appropriately. Some of us have old fears from parent-child relationships, and some of us still don't know how to say "no" to Mom and Dad. The word "no" is not disrespectful, and we need not perceive it as such. As adults we should be free to make up our own minds and say what we feel in a respectful way. These childhood fears must be confronted, for they leave room and building blocks for greater fears.

Spiritual fears involve the concept that God is going to catch an individual in wrongdoings. Taking responsibility and practicing the living Word will remove fears. For instance, having faith and respect for God will help a person to do what God commands instead of fearing the result of disobeying his Word. When a person is responsible and does what he or she should do, there is no need to fear. If you have spiritual fears, make up your mind to do what is written instead of choosing to have fear. Having faith in God will combat fear.

When a person has strong beliefs in God they are convinced that there is a guardian angel watching over them who will take over when they are unable to perform. Such belief in a higher power gives them a kind of relief and a positive outlook on situations that seem impossible. Relief also comes because the individual feels that God will help them, He will put good people in their paths and He will guide them in making good decisions. They also believe that God will give them strength when they are weak. Prayer, therefore, is a great weapon to be used in your life to relieve fears.

The fear of success is another fear that is very common in some environments. This fear exists because success is a big responsibility; therefore those who fear success, fear responsibility. However, the responsibility that comes with being successful is still the opportunity of a lifetime to grow and to learn, and success will open doors that have never been opened before.

Financial success allows you to be able to afford the finer things in life. Therefore, people who fear success should have faith in themselves and believe that if they can reach success they can do what it takes to stay successful. The fear of success also happens when you speculate and look too far into the future. However, knock down this fear by taking one day at a time and enjoying the moment. Talk to, read about, or write letters to successful people. Get an idea of what they have gone through to gain a successful life. Most people who have become successful have no desire to trade places with an unsuccessful person. Just the opposite is true: they love their success. This gives me the idea that there must be something very nice about being successful. So go for it!

Fear for the sake of fear is when an individual holds on to fear and becomes comfortable in their fear. This individual fears everything in life and won't attempt to do anything, even things that require little effort. They even fear when they are not doing anything. They become a sitting duck and believe that everyone except them can accomplish their goals. This kind of fear is overcome by confrontation. This person who just fears for the sake of fear can make a chart and write down their fears on paper. They can also write down the methods that they need to use to overcome these fears. Gradually, they can make changes by using the methods illustrated on the charts that they have made. By the way, also consider this question--are these fears realistic? If the answer is no, or even if the answer is a whopping yes---begin to knock down your fears.

Confront and conquer your fears by acknowledging them. Be honest about them and every day do something to knock them down. If there is no threat or physical challenge, gradually move in on your fears at a very slow pace. Ask loved ones to help you deal with these fears on a consistent basis.

Notes

3 BECOME A CREATOR

A person must have faith in divine authority, God, and believe that we were all made by His creative power. After God made man and woman through his creative power, he distributed his creativity to each individual. The challenge is for you to believe and then discover the creativity that is within you.

WHAT IS CREATIVITY?

The dictionary defines creativity as (1) being productive, (2) having the power or quality of creating, (3) the ability to make or create, or originality. I must conclude from these definitions that creativity is an in-born and innate talent that must be cultivated, shaped and directed. Therefore, you must be aware of your own creativity and then nurture it. It should be each individual's goal to find their secret talent that God chose to give to them. You should become very curious and motivated to know why God would place such a talent in your life. You should be motivated to find this talent and to use it effectively.

How Can You Discover Your Creativity?

One of the most effective ways to find answers is to ask pertinent questions. A scientist makes each scientific breakthrough by using the scientific method. They form a theory as an example, ask specific questions, and then test their theory and answers. Utilize the scientific method to help you find your creativity. Do this by asking yourself germane questions. Ask yourself questions such as what do I like to do? Answer this question on paper. For instance, if you love to draw, ask yourself if you are good at drawing. Also, ask yourself if it feels almost effortless for you to draw even though it is a lot of hard work. Remember to also ask yourself this most important question in order to discover your creativity: What is it that I love to do so much that if I didn't get paid I would still do it?

If you find this process difficult and if you need support finding your creativity, then ask a close, honest, and sincere family member or friend to help you answer these questions about you. Ask them to help you find your creativity by making a list of the things that they feel that you can perform very well. Do this exercise on paper. Now, you and your friend should enjoy making a list of your positive characteristics on paper. For example, if you love to talk and you do so very well, then you may want to examine the communications field and put this on your list. Allow your close family or close friends to help you make your list so that your list is accurate and honest. Your family and friends can help to point you toward your creativity.

Another method that you can use to discover your creativity is to embark upon new ventures. Sometimes the best way to find out if you truly like something is by doing it. You can volunteer to do various things to help you find your likes, dislikes, and creativity. Trying new and positive ideas and seeing how you enjoy doing them can also help you in this endeavor. For example, find out if a sewing class is being offered at a college in your neighborhood, and then take the class to see if one of your creative areas is sewing. Involving yourself in various creative activities on a regular basis will help you obtain balance and diversity. This will also prevent you from becoming locked into a stagnated routine that just leads you to work and back home again. This will help to stir up your creativity, which releases creative energy.

Examine books from the library; read and learn about new, exciting, popular, and fascinating ideas. I don't suggest that you try everything that you read. As you read and search for your creativity, be selective and choose something that is of great interest to you. Also, read your newspaper and get acquainted with different activities in your community. You may not be able to become very involved in every activity, but maybe you can begin by doing activities once a month. You may find out your creative direction by interacting with people and by being involved in your community. Interacting with a variety of people may help creative juices begin to flow more often.

Another way to search for your creativity is to examine your family tree and your immediate family members. Ask questions about what they did for a living and what they did for fun. Sometimes creativity is hereditary, and you could have inherited creative traits from your great-grandparents. Consider excellent teachers as a good source of discovering your creativity.

They can at times notice special talents. The key is to make your inquires from a teacher who cares about you, who is knowledgeable, and who is very positive. Be determined and inventive to find ways that will inform you of your creativity. When your creativity comes forth it is obvious to everyone because there is something beautiful and special about it.

CREATIVITY VERSUS EDUCATION

We live in a society that almost demands that in order to be heard or to be acknowledged we must hold some sort of degree. It is needful that we seek some level of education and pursue it. Creativity should never be an enemy of education. In other words, education and creativity must complement each other. An individual should be educated and creative at the same time. The dictionary defines education as the field of study that deals mainly with methods of teaching and learning in schools or the knowledge and development resulting from an educational process.

I will at this point summarize these definitions for you and say in my own words that education is an accumulation of experiences, principles, knowledge, and patterns that are taught by someone or by life itself. In our society most people attend a formal school setting or home study program to learn what we call book knowledge. Also, some of the most valuable knowledge is gained through job experience or life's hard knocks. All of these methods are inclusive in the process of learning. When applied appropriately, education will broaden your scope of thinking and will make a person more flexible in their lives.

Education is not supposed to make a person feel superior, but it should assist a person's mind in allowing them to communicate to others and to understand others more completely. When education is applied to a person's life properly, it makes them more humble, quiet, confident and understanding. Instead of an individual becoming obsessed with elaborate vocabulary, education should open the channel for him to be able to choose words and shape phrases simply enough for everyone. Education helps to manage creativity. An individual who is truly educated has no need to flaunt his education since knowledge should be shared among all people. Once a person becomes educated they have a responsibility to share their knowledge. On the other hand, a person can be theoretically educated but remain stupid in the manner in which they choose to handle their education. Your education should open a door for your creativity. Your creativity can lead you to obtain an education to further enhance more creativity. Therefore, education and creativity are companions and they work together.

Notes

4 POWER

Various people interpret power differently. Even the dictionary expresses multiple meanings when the word power is defined. Therefore, power is easily misunderstood and vastly abused by many people. The majority of our society is excited about power and misuses power. Our society wants to use power, yet they do not clearly understand the total characteristics of power. This word, alone, is impressive by itself. Its significance is outstanding. It leaves a lasting mental and emotional image.

This word is intensely forceful. It stimulates the mental and emotional processes of everyone, and in many different ways. Even a young child will react when the word is used. They might raise a hand as a symbol of power. Society acknowledges this word and consciously and subconsciously responds to it by letting this word be manifest in daily life. This chapter will express the extensive use of the word *power*. We will examine some new perceptions of power. We will bring the word power to a precise point and satisfy the audience with a clear focus on this magnificent word.

Most of us have heard the phrase "world power" discussed in our history classes. We have heard this phrase spoken by our politicians. Our political system is such that we elect politicians who we sincerely believe will make our country achieve and maintain "world power." We have established a world in which most countries choose to utilize their monies to develop their military system in an effort to have "world power." They choose to do this rather than choosing to have human dignity and choosing to feed their starving populations. Some choose to have "world power" by neglecting the poor, ignoring the need for health insurance for working people, and by allowing a vast number of the population of children to be unable to obtain inoculation against childhood diseases.

In some cases the smallest of nations have competed and fought wars against the largest counties. They do this to be included, acknowledged, and recognized in society as having some kind of "world power." Regardless of how poor and how small a country may be, "world power" is at the top of their wish-list of achievements. For example, the Russians insisted on having "world power" while their economy was privately declining. Instead, they surprised the world with a collapsed economy and a nation of starving people. Still, our historians, and politicians have not clearly and specifically gotten the point.

The fact is that "world power" does not exist when there is a lack of individual education, a lack of individual dignity and a failure to meet individual basic needs. The Russians have shown us that "world power" is a false front waiting to collapse. This collapse happens when a vast number of the population is hungry, homeless, jobless, drug addicted, hurting, and filled with emotional pain. This can be no claim to power! Also "world power" is an ingenious front waiting to collapse when our population is unhappy and our youth are becoming lost, misguided, dreamless, and when they lack enthusiasm for the future. It is incumbent upon our educators, historians, politicians, and all of us to re-evaluate and exclusively define the word "power" and put it in perspective.

Women have also experienced the misuse and the misunderstanding of the word power. Men have believed that in order to feel powerful they must dominate women. To men, this kind of domination meant that men gave instructions about everything and women followed their instructions. For decades society has been confused about power as it relates to women. It took centuries for society to acknowledge the wisdom that women have to offer and the rights that a woman must exercise in order to put her wisdom to full usage.

Therefore society has missed out on the diversity provided by women and they have tremendous problems in trying to balance the forces of women and men to equal power. It took centuries for the world to realize that letting a woman have her rights does not take away from a man's rights. A woman exercising her self-awareness does not make a man powerless. The misconception of the word power in this way has led to women being abused in society. Society has felt for years that in order to have power, somebody or something must be suppressed, hurt, or beaten.

Since most people are acquainted with the dictionary, we will begin with a look at definitions from Webster's dictionary. Power is defined as (1) possession of control; (2) authority, or influence over others; (3) the ability to act or produce an effect; (4) physical might; (5) mental or moral efficiency, and (6) political control or influence. These definitions will have surprised some of us. Most of us may have assumed that we knew the definition of power and never even bothered to look up this word in the dictionary.

The one word that will immensely modify these remarkable definitions by Webster is "self." I would   presume to say that Webster must have thought that the word "self" would be automatically implied by everyone who read these definitions. The first definition states that power is possession of control. In order to truly have possession of control you must have possession of control of yourself. All of the definitions that Webster gave are true and effective if you begin with "self" and end with "self." I would surmise from the definitions that power is when people take a look inside themselves and initiate discipline at all times, which is being in total control of one's self.

This involves influencing others and being a model with the real ability to say "no" to all destructive thoughts, emotions, and outside forces and to say "yes" to everything positive. Contrary to popular opinion, power is not external; power is internal. Power is being able to use your own unique discretion to select love, peace, and everything good over corruption, evil and all things negative. Power is having emotional, physical, and psychological control of yourself and having the spiritual awareness of your likeness to the most powerful God.

Genesis 1:26 tells us that the Almighty God created man in his own likeness. God is all-powerful and man/woman has the ability to be innately powerful. However an individual must be spiritually aware of where power comes from, what power really means, who gives power, and how to obtain power. In order to obtain power a person must first look inside his or herself and reveal his or her own fears, insecurities, doubts, faults, and pain and with great determination annihilate them.

You cannot destroy such power blockers by blaming someone else for them or by ignoring them. These power blockers must be discovered and they must be conquered. We very often search for someone who is weak to dominate him or her instead of searching out ourselves. By doing this we believe that power is achieved by domination, but it is not. Such an implication is untrue, and eventually such actions and implications lead to a greater insecurity in individuals.

Be mindful that a powerful person will always be true to himself and is honest about his own growth and development. An individual who wants power does not achieve it by beating down his neighbor and by being jealous of others, nor does he achieve personal power by suppressing his fellow man. Power cannot be maintained by suppression. It is only fear, internal conflicts, insecurity, and powerlessness that perpetuate suppression. The person who is attempting suppression and control of others is a weak and insecure individual. Remember, that which is meant to be great cannot be suppressed indefinitely but must eventually rise to the top. Suppression is a waste of the oppressor's time and can make the person being suppressed become more resilient.

On the other hand, if you exercise true power you will not have the space or the time for other negative and unlawful behaviors such as domination and suppression. A person who is always striking out at someone is feeling powerless and lacks control of his own being and his immediate surroundings. A person who is truly powerful and authoritative can withhold (control) himself from striking out or even annihilating his enemy; instead he will exercise the power to refrain. By this I don't mean to hold anger and other emotions inside and become sick. Power is real, it is not pretense. For example, God himself who is all-powerful has the power to destroy everyone who disobeys him, but instead he refrains. God has the power to make all creatures and creation serve him, but he refrains. Mankind must also exemplify power by being able to constrain themselves and their emotions. A person who is a bully, who intimidates and tries to control others, is powerless and is out of self-control.

Power is knowledge. Power is the knowledge that you have accumulated about yourself concerning your strengths and your weaknesses. Power is when you have come to know how to manage those weaknesses and those strengths. Power is the knowledge that you have about others, your environment, your subject and most of all, the knowledge that you have of your relationship with your maker: God. Power is the knowledge that you have gained on how to improve yourself and your immediate surroundings. Power is the influence that you have in your community due to the knowledge and the awareness that you have gained and are able to impart. Power is the knowledge that you are able to leave imprinted on the minds of your children, friends, and extended family. Power is the good that you know, power is the good that you know and are willing to share. Power does not need to be shown negatively, but power is a positive force that will uplift a person from the bottom of life to the top of life. He who has power can uplift people with words and with the power of love.

Develop these characteristics below and possess internal power

Be humble
Be merciful unto others
Be teachable
Be able to absorb knowledge
Be able to apply knowledge and wisdom to situations
Be confident in everything that you do
Be able to accept constructive criticism
Be determined
Be flexible
Be willing to change the things that do not work
Dare to be original
Be able to do honest self-assessment

Self-Evaluation:

A. Put a star by the above characteristics that you already possess.
B. Put a happy face by the characteristics that you need to improve, and remember to smile as you work hard to improve them.
C. Create your own list of characteristics that you need to improve.

Resist the urge to practice these <u>pseudo-power</u> characteristics below:

Suppressing others
Gossiping and labeling people
Selfishness
Hate
Malice
Jealousy
Argumentativeness
Demeaning others
Disrespectfulness
Attention seeking
Pretentiousness
Lying and untruthfulness
Laziness
Misusing and abusing others; gaming
Manipulation
Underestimating others
Overestimating yourself
Displaying the need for compliments
Physical fighting
Intimidation
Bullying

A. Mentally, spiritually, emotionally and psychologically remove your *pseudo-power* characteristics by confessing them in the space provided.
B. List positive characteristics that you will use to replace the ones that you confessed.
C. Re-read this chapter after these exercises.

Notes

5 THE POWER OF LOVE

I believe that love is a positive and a strong motivator that gives us the strength and the power to overcome every obstacle that is in our way.

THE LOVE OF GOD

The love of God in a person's heart is demonstrated when the person shows total respect toward everything that is made by God. It is demonstrated when the person knows that God is the Supreme Being in his heart, and when the person shows reverence toward all of God's creation. When the love of God is in a person's heart, the most important thing to the person is what God says, what God feels, and what God knows about any situation. Therefore, with this kind of love operating, this person can only make positive decisions and use accurate judgment, because all decisions are based on God's feelings or how an individual feels about God.

On the other hand, without this love a person has no morals, and without morals this person has no conscience. Therefore, this person will do anything and will disrespect anyone, because they have no righteous guilt or consciousness. An individual with this attitude adversely affects himself or herself and destroys their own opportunity to achieve. This negative attitude therefore disarms this individual and puts the individual at war with himself or herself. The negativity heightens and the individual began to be at war with everyone. Also, when the love of God does not abide in a person's heart a void is present which will be filled with another negative emotion like hate or anger. In other words, the more love you have in your heart the less room you have for hate, hurt, and for other negative emotions. It becomes clear that a person positions himself to fail at his endeavors when he does not love God. Therefore it is necessary to find the love of God and possess it in your heart in order to find yourself and live your life to the fullest.

When a person loves God then the door is open for him to love that which God has created, which is himself and his fellowman. This love will cause this person to emotionally become the healthiest human being, a great family person, and a best friend. One disadvantage to society is that many people keep this love suppressed and trapped inside. People are afraid that if they express this love that others will mistake it for weakness. However, when a person suppresses this powerful love it prevents him from feeling and sharing ultimate joy. It also prevents this person from feeling a certain fulfillment in life. The love of God in a person's heart must be released freely and must be enjoyed by others. When a person experiences the power of the love of God that is released, then they are sharing in the pleasure and in the sweetness of love. This love must be released into the environment because it is like a magnet; when it is released it pulls positivity, joy, and peace towards us all.

In order to show love we must clearly understand what love is and how love is demonstrated. Love is strong and love opposes weakness. Therefore, love does not mean that you allow someone to virtually 'walk all over your feelings'. Neither does love mean that you allow others to abuse your rights as an individual. The fact of the matter is that love sets boundaries. Love upholds certain principles and love earns and demands respect. Love is strong and courageous. When a person's heart is full of love they cannot accept or give in to disrespect from anyone. The love in a person gives respect, and it demands respect in return. The love in a person is tolerant of others but does not accept wrong. Instead, that love sets and holds everyone to a standard of righteousness and truth. Love is brave. However, a person must first love himself or herself before they can love or have love with anyone else.

If you cannot love and appreciate yourself, how can you see the beauty in others and how can you love and appreciate others? The fact that a person cannot love himself will always stand in the way of him loving others. However, if an individual loves God and sees himself in God's image or likeness, it becomes easier for him to love himself. Adversely, if an individual still continues to have difficulty loving himself, he can look at himself and set a standard of good principles and character and radiate love from the inside first. If unfavorable characteristics are still present, then the individual can change those characteristics so that love for himself can generate and grow from within and not from without.

After a person loves himself for who he is internally, then he can love himself externally. Also, he can learn to appreciate and to love the uniqueness that God molded his features into, by noticing the beauty and the resemblance of special family members, and love this beauty. Start by loving your mother and father just for making it possible for you to enter the universe. If your parents gave you away or even dumped you, it doesn't matter; just love the fact that they came together and made you. Be thankful, and love the fact that you are here and that you are in control of loving yourself. You are now responsible for your outcome and you are responsible to love yourself and to love others.

You have so much to love for, and this love feels so good that you have neither the time nor the purpose to hate. It is so much easier and nicer to let go of hate, jealously and other negative forces and to just love yourself and others. When you can see yourself as a love-producing human being with lots of love to give, and you can see beauty in yourself and in others, then it's easier for you to love yourself and others. The ability to love others is evident when you have introduced yourself to the love of God. After you have experienced the love of God, then you know how sweet and how secure love is and you become willing to expose others to this kind of love.

Love deals with the heart and love produces life-giving actions. When a person says with their mouth that they have love, their actions must always show that same love. We must understand that love is a deed; it's what you do and not just what you say. When you have love, you will not knowingly hurt someone but you will always seek to better that someone's circumstances. If you are associated with someone who is always hurting you but who says that they love you, I question that love. Love comes from the heart and it produces good and healthy actions.

Since we are humans, we are fallible. Therefore, we make mistakes. However, there is a difference between making a mistake and doing something that you know will hurt someone. When we have love within us it makes us conscious of other people's feelings and emotions. It makes us operate our lives well with great respect for ourselves and great respect for others. Love warrants ultimate respect both from the recipient and from the giver.

When love is shown it makes an enormous difference. Love for yourself allows you to profoundly care for your body holistically. This kind of love will not accept anything other than love and will not dispense anything other than more love. Love cannot be fooled. When a person has love they can identify when love is around them. Love either exists around you or it doesn't. However, in order for you to rise from the things that keep you down you must first love God, then love yourself, and then love your fellow man. It must be in this order.

I have expounded on and I have emphasized self-love in detail, but there is a great difference between self-love and selfishness. Love cannot be selfish because love knows how to divide and how to share equally. When a person is selfish they are afraid that if they don't take all or most for themselves, they will never get anything. Therefore, a selfish person is an insecure and a fearful person. Love gives and love receives equally. Love brings about freedom, and this includes the freedom to give, to let go, and to share. Love gives you conquering power over your own life.

Love is not lifted up and love is not boastful of self. Love enables you to see yourself as the wonderful work of God's hands. Thereby you are always proud of God and the continuous work that he allows you to do on yourself. When a person is secure in this knowledge it gives him power to change unfavorable situations. This kind of love will always search for the opportunity to spread itself instead of just the opportunity to receive. Love is contagious and love is very unselfish. When you love God you can see God in his glory and you can see the mere fact that you can never fail at anything if you continue to love God. Now your success in life becomes dependent on the power of God's love for mankind instead of on your little strength. Now, you are assured that God will love you because you love him.

Love releases power and positivity, and this power is not dormant. Love produces seeds of truth and honesty. You cannot remain around love and not be affected. Remember; while you love someone, God and others love you. An individual who has love possesses great power to achieve and to draw positive forces to themselves. On the other hand, an individual who has hate or anger possesses greater power to destroy themselves and others. One who has no love has no positive power. However, those who don't know about love must learn about love. It is our responsibility to seek out people who have love and who can also return love to us. We must incorporate people into our lives who can give and who can receive care and love. We must have people around us who have love and to whom we enjoy giving our love. We need love, and we need to give love.

1 CORINTHIANS 13 (KING JAMES VERSION)

Though I speak with the tongues of men and of angels, and have not charity, I am become as sounding brass, or a tinkling cymbal.

And though I have the gift of prophecy, and understand all mysteries, and all knowledge; and though I have all faith, so that I could remove mountains, and have not charity, I am nothing.

And though I bestow all my goods to feed the poor, and tough I give my body to be burned, and have not charity, it profiteth me nothing.

Charity suffereth long, and is kind; charity envieth not; charity vaunteth not itself, is not puffed up.

Doth not behave itself unseemly, seeketh not her own, is not easily provoked, thinketh no evil; Rejoiceth not in iniquity, but rejoiceth in the truth; Beareth all things, believeth all things, hopeth all things, endureth all things.

Charity never faileth: but whether there be prophecies, they shall fail; whether there be tongues, they shall cease; whether there be knowledge, it shall vanish away.

For we know in part, and we prophesy in part. But when that which is perfect is come, then that which is in part shall be done away.

When I was a child, I spake as a child, I understood as a child, I thought as a child: but when I became a man, I put away childish things.

For now we see through a glass, darkly; but then face to face: now I know in part; but then shall I know even as also I am known.

And now abideth faith, hope, charity, these three; but the greatest of these is charity.

Notes

6 HOW TO KEEP YOUR MAN

Ever since the beginning of time there have been difficulties in the relationships between men and women. Adam and Eve first disagreed about eating the fruit of the tree of knowledge. They disagreed about their explanation of the reasons why they ate the fruit. These arguments have continued throughout the centuries, and men and women are still struggling to agree today. The fact is that men and women are made different physically, emotionally, and psychologically, and society is guilty of capitalizing on these differences.

Far too long women have experienced the disadvantage in the relationship between men and women. Women have endlessly searched for a bridging of the gap between themselves and the men in their lives. Men have enjoyed women's inability to discover men's mysteries. Some brilliant women concluded that the relationship between men and women can't work well until it is balanced. This means that women must become equal partners in their relationships. On the other hand some men, but not all men are continuing to attempt to keep a certain psychological and emotional control.

This psychological and emotional control pressures women into feeling that their role is to serve men, deliver sex to men, sacrifice for men, and I could list many more items. A woman must find a solution to the gender war, and she begins by first loving herself. In so many relationships the man just receives love and the woman keeps on giving love. The man has no reason to change because he has the woman fulfilling all of his needs and putting his needs before hers; therefore, he keeps her in this position to assure that his needs are met.

Men figured out a long time ago how to keep women emotionally dependent and how to keep them coming back for more false love. On the other hand, some women have surrendered their lives to the man that they are in a relationship with, and now women have discovered that making these sacrifices for men doesn't win men over. These sacrifices only encourage some men to take advantage of the kindness of women.

The act of loving a man more than you love yourself gives him the luxury of always disrespecting you, using you, and taking you for granted. Loving a man should not make a woman lose control of herself, because when she is in a state of 'lack of control' she is weak and vulnerable. Love cannot grow in a weak and vulnerable relationship.

Love needs a strong and a balanced relationship in order to flourish and to thrive. In order to have a healthy relationship the woman must love herself above all, thereby indicating to the man that she will not settle for less from him than what she offers herself. Therefore, she shows the man how to love and how to care for her by the manner in which she loves and cares for herself. She must create a standard of love from which she will never deviate under any circumstances. Chances are that he will treat her as well as she treats herself.

A man cannot fulfill the role of making a woman happy. This is a role that every woman must learn to achieve for herself. She needs to explore herself to find the sources of her happiness. She needs to demand that as a man receives love from the relationship, he also gives to her these elements that add to her happiness in return. If she knows how to make herself happy, then she can communicate the sources of her happiness to him so that they can be happy together and they can have a healthy relationship.

However, if she remains at an emotional disadvantage, begging him for his time and his attention, some men will keep her on her hands and her knees and enjoy her sacrifices and endeavors to draw him to her. Most men are not as naive as women think; some men conquer women in the area of relationships and they find ways to meet and to satisfy their needs all of the time. They find escape from the burdens of families, relationships, and life as a whole while many women nag, cry, and chase them. Some men enjoy the game of 'catch me if you can!'

A woman loving herself does not mean selfishness or self-centeredness. These two negative behaviors tip the scale and they are the result of some kind of emotional instability. They do not benefit the woman in the long term. The concept of a woman loving herself first simply refers to her not allowing a man to put his needs above hers. Instead, she provides for fairness in meeting each other's needs. It means that she respects herself so much that she will never tolerate any disrespect from any man, although he might be 'every woman's dream.' This man is not best for her if he cannot give her the required essentials of a relationship.

A woman loving herself means letting a man know that she is expecting satisfaction out of the relationship and holding him to this commitment. Many immature men have come to feel that a relationship means getting all of the sex that they need, when they need it, without romance or emotional completeness for the woman. However, when a woman loves herself she takes responsibility for the relationship and she will not put the relationship in an immature man's hands to let him play his games. Love is not blind. Love is sensible and only weakness and low self-esteem is blind.

A man enters a relationship with vigor. He stresses his desires, whether they are sex, a long-term relationship, or a good time. Women of all colors and ages must take notice and not be afraid to do the same thing: Stress what you want in a relationship and make sure that it is received. Loving yourself means taking care of yourself. It also means not allowing anyone to abuse or to disrespect your rights in a friendship or a romantic relationship. Some men use their power of persuasion. They utilize this power all of the time to get jobs, dates, or to have sex.

The point is, they use it in every aspect of their lives. While some men dominate in the use of their power of persuasion, some women feel uneasy or think that it is deceitful to use persuasion in relationships. The art of using the power of persuasion germinates by practice, and women must learn it effectively so that they can persuade men to take them seriously in relationships. Women must be able to use silence, talking, writing, body language and appearance to persuade men to respect them and to meet the standard that they set in a relationship. Women, keeping your man means having your man care for you! If you have started out a relationship wrong, make a fresh start and don't wait for him to change; you start your change of self-love, self-respect and persuasion.

Women complain that some men don't talk enough. This phrase could be interpreted to mean that women talk too much. When we women constantly take responsibility for conversations, we indirectly give men an escape or reason not to talk. What do you think would happen if a woman sat silently on the couch beside a quiet spouse and flicked the T.V. off? How would a quiet spouse react to complete silence when the woman doesn't show any interest in initiating a conversation?

If a woman keeps quiet, a silent spouse would probably think that she has lost her mind for not talking to him. When a woman is flexible and has learned when and how to be silent, she is able to encourage the man to participate in initiating conversation. Most men only understand and perceive action, and they ignore unpersuasive threats, talking and complaining. At times it might be necessary to talk less and to act more. You can have him communicate with you better. Some men also use the newspaper, TV, friends, and sports as a way of escaping communication and responsibilities. Some men are obsessed with these escape mechanisms and they need professional help---or, they may just need to be single. However, the majority of men can put the newspaper, TV, friends, and sports into perspective. Most women accept and tolerate the ways that men abuse the methods of escape, therefore men just keep on escaping and avoiding the work that their relationship needs. These techniques become men's outlet or a method of avoiding communication. For decades, women have thought that men 'just didn't get it,' but they got it a long time ago. They are just very good at taking care of their own needs despite the consequences.

Men use their minds and not their emotions, while women use their emotions most of the time when they should be using their minds. What would happen if the women beat the men in grabbing the newspaper in the a.m. or in the p.m. and practiced his silent method? What would happen if she beat him at watching the games and screamed louder than he does? Most men when they see themselves through the actions of their spouse become annoyed. What if whatever he does to annoy her, she can do better? Who would be annoyed then? Many times, complaining or a woman's manner of communicating can be negative attention for men. What if women competed with men and beat them at their own game? Women must avoid the habit of being taken for granted.

We make the mistake of making the kitchen the center of attention for the man. One of the first things most women want a man to know is how well she can 'burn' in the kitchen. Believe me, he will never forget it, but instead of going out to dinner he will want you to continue to 'burn' in the kitchen. It's a good idea for all women to have a restaurant day per month where the family eats out and she doesn't have to do the cooking. If he can't afford it she should squeeze it into the budget. When the woman is doing the cooking she should cook what she likes to eat mostly and cook what he likes sometimes. She should not spend most of her time trying to tantalize his taste buds, because she could set herself up for disaster. In other words, cook at the average so that he will appreciate and enjoy it but not demand and expect it.

Most men think that a woman's place is in the kitchen, so let him get in the kitchen enough so that he will feel comfortable there. Due to this myth, the kitchen has replaced the bedroom, and some men prefer their spouse's cooking to their spouse's romance and sex. This myth must be erased. A woman must accept and she must enjoy her freedom just as a man has done. We also sometimes send the message that our place is in the kitchen when we allow them to go and play or enjoy themselves while we stay home and cook. When this occurs, we confirm their belief that we are happy in the kitchen, and that the kitchen is our only interest. I am not implying that we should lose our love of cooking. For example, if we go out and play at the same time they do and cook something special afterward, expressing the thought that we are cooking because we feel like eating something special there will be no misunderstanding.

Women must know that self-gratification feels very nice in a relationship. If there is any doubt about this fact, just ask some men, because some men enjoy it all of the time. It feels so good to get what you want out of a relationship and to keep him pleasing you as you please him. Remember that as long as you are getting what you want out of the relationship, you can give him what he needs. Sex is an important part of a relationship and women have been through a sexual revolution.

On the other hand, some men have always received the ultimate sexual experience. Some immature men even thought that they owned sex and that sex was made for them. In today's society a woman has come to know that she should have sex if she desires it and not just at the drop of an immature man's pants. Sometimes it is even good to say "no" and to keep him in suspense. Some immature men usually have a big ego that needs to be stroked at times, but most times their big ego needs to be deflated. When his ego is deflated, you have done him a favor. Let me explain……

A woman must never become predictable, nice, and easy. Make your partner work for the relationship that is worth keeping. He works for anything else that is of value to him, and if he becomes complacent he loses it. He must be cognizant that if he refuses to do everything possible for your relationship, he will lose it also. Why do women give men so much 'slack' when it comes to relationships? If you want to keep him you must keep him working on the relationship and appreciating you. Be gentle, yet demanding. The more active a man is in giving flowers and romance, the easier it is to do. The above principles apply to everything in life. It is harder to revive something than it is to keep it alive. However, if you keep your relationship alive you won't ever have to revive it.

Keeping the relationship fresh does not mean that the woman does all of the work. However, she is mostly responsible for working on herself. She must be certain that she does not become stagnated, unhappy, bored, or have a feeling of low self-esteem in any relationship. She must be alert and in tune enough with herself to know if her needs are satisfied. This may sound hard or sound like it's a lot of work. On the other hand, these responsibilities should be pleasurable and not a burden. After all, some women have been ensuring that some men's needs were met for centuries, which did not seem to be too hard to do. Therefore, it should not be too hard for women to now ensure that their own needs are met every day.

When monitoring your relationship daily, put the reality ahead of your emotions. Don't make excuses for mistreatment from a spouse, but acknowledge the facts and deal with them appropriately. A word of caution: If you are one of those women who are not being gratified, make gradual changes and then as the relationship gets stronger make more serious changes. If you do not want to risk the relationship, make changes that the relationship can endure at the beginning and then move on slowly to greater changes. However, no one should have to settle for unhappiness or for a sick, unhealthy relationship.

Let the person who is happy be you. Give as much as you get, because you are special and you should be treated wonderfully. It doesn't matter your size, color or what features you have; a man should give you ultimate love and respect. Your relationship should be enjoyable the majority of times. Since you cannot depend on a man to make you happy, you should be able to depend on yourself not to allow a man to make you unhappy.

A healthy relationship between a man and a woman is wholesome in all aspects. This relationship makes the woman feel that she is the most important person in the world. Honesty is foremost and faithfulness is a must. A man and a woman are able to share each other solely and to share each other at the highest level of sharing. He should be able to enjoy the most intimate part of her being and she should be able to reach him to the deepest degree. Each should be so taken with the other that if the most outstanding model stands before them undressed, they should look around the model for each other, since each is moved deeply only by the other.

In a healthy relationship both partners are equal and see each other as such. They are willing to support each other in every form of work and in every goal pursued. There is no great amount of jealously and envy, but they hold complete good wishes for each other. When one partner is hurt the other partner feels the same pain. There is therefore no space or room for someone else to enter a healthy relationship, except in friendship. Although these friends are on the outside, they are not able to trouble the relationship in any way. Men and women can share each other to the degree that God intended. Whenever there is a disagreement, each partner is eager to reconcile the argument and they have no hesitation to apologize if they are wrong.

Listening is vital in a healthy relationship. Each partner hears and tries hard to understand the other, and they treat each other's point of view with great respect. The communication is never one-sided, but the couple talks to and with each other. Time is set aside for each other no matter how busy the day gets. Sex is not an obligation for the woman, but both partners desire each other in the same way and they enjoy their sex life. The woman is romanced enough that she wants to have sex with her partner. Sex is not a chore but is an emotional, psychological and physical thrill for both partners. A healthy relationship feels good and does not cause pain. It contributes joy, gladness, and happiness to your life, and not grief. No woman should settle for anything other than a healthy and a fulfilling relationship.

Women have felt the pressure to get a man and to keep a man. Women have tried to be what men are looking for and women have made great efforts to make their appearance attractive for men. The enormous pressure of taking care of a family, maintaining a stable job, and other stress has contributed to some women becoming overweight, unhappy, and being overly concerned about looking the way that they think men want them to look. In other words, women allow the desire of some men to dictate their appearance and their apparel.

We must get back to being ourselves, enjoying ourselves, dressing for the occasion, and we must not just spend our time trying to please men's sense of what they think looks good. In an attempt to look attractive for men some women have allowed the sexual appetite of men to define sexiness and attractiveness. Therefore, many young girls and young adults have resorted to wearing almost no clothes at all, exposing the most precious and private parts of their bodies in order to please men. In society, modesty has taken an exit and a cheapened appearance is dominant. Some men gives a nod of approval, an eye wink, or some kind of inappropriate comment when a woman is fully exposed and thinks that she is sexy or that she is exhibiting sex appeal. Sometimes, a man will try to start some jealousy between women by indirectly approving of a loosely dressed woman when they are around a more conservatively dressed woman.

Women, take a look around your environment; do you see men walking around with pants so tight that you can see the imprint of their scrotum or penis? Do you see them exposing their chest so that you can determine the size of it? Are they wearing shorts so short that their pubic hairs are exposed? Only women can affect a change in this double standard. Until women begin to demand that they are taken seriously and that they are looked upon holistically instead of as sex objects; men will continue to have this appetite and they will take advantage of women's desire to satisfy them.

We should dress appropriately for the weather, for the occasion and for ourselves. We should not dress to turn men on or to satisfy men's sexual urges. When we dress to satisfy the sexual desires of men we disrespect our bodies, our womanhood, and ourselves in order to meet a distorted concept of what they deemed attractive or sexy. Therefore, our daughters are going to school thinking that being sexy is being naked. Boys are able to pressure girls very easily because of the fragile concept that we have given girls. It does not benefit a woman to attract a man because he had an open view of her exposed breast, abdomen, and buttocks on the first or second meeting. A woman can be attractive, sexy and modest.

Being hoochie should be left for those in the videos, but women on these videos must also stop allowing men to use them to sell their products. Men are having a cheap good time and we are supplying the demand. Therefore, do not give them a cheap eye full of lust and be confident that they are capable of having compliant behavior. The next time that you step outside of your doors look into the mirror carefully and be sure that the way that you look is the way that you want to be perceived and remembered. Personal hygiene must never lag behind in your personal life or in your relationship. You must be sure not to become so overwhelmed with other responsibilities and forget about your personal hygiene.

Enjoy your feminism and take special care of your body. Soap and warm water are the best solution to prevent hygiene problems. For women this means to cleanse the body thoroughly several times throughout the day. A complete bath or shower includes thorough cleaning. Begin by flossing the teeth and getting between the gums completely. Use plenty of warm water to rinse the gums after flossing. Use a tooth powder sold at health food stores to brush the teeth. Brush away from the gums. Use a tongue apparatus sold at stores or use your toothbrush to brush and clean the tongue. Then use your favorite toothpaste and mouthwash. Also, remember that it is recommended that you floss after every meal to prevent halitosis. It is also recommended that you visit your dentist every six months for dental care.

Wash the face with a face wash such as Ester C, patting the face dry and applying moisturizer. Use the same care you use on your face for your neck. Continue by using plenty of warm water, wetting a clean soft washcloth and creating lots of suds with your preferable moisturizing soap. Take good care to throw away all old washcloths and use a clean dry and fresh washcloth for every washing and cleansing. Use the soapy washcloth on your upper torso in circular motion. Lift up the breast, wash under the breast and the nipples, and wash the abdomen and belly button which is your umbilicus. Wash both arms and underarms with circular motions.

Rinse the washcloth thoroughly, then re-soap it thoroughly and wash the thighs, lower legs, and feet including between the toes and heels. Also, rinse the washcloth thoroughly and then re-soap it and wash the entire back. You may rinse the washcloth again or you may use a new washcloth. Soap another washcloth with lots of soap creating suds and wash the vagina. Separate the labia or the lips of the vagina and wash it well. Separate the buttock cheeks and be sure to wash the anus. Be sure to allow enough warm water to run freely by separating all folds with your hands. Soap and warm water should reach all external areas of the perineum and the entire body.

After showering use a clean dry towel to pat the body dry. Be sure to dry the perineum area and the underarms well because if they are not dried well the moisture and wetness will create unpleasant odor. Apply body lotion to the areas of your choosing. Some people apply lotion to the entire body to keep the skin moist and youthful. Several parts of the body that we neglect are the external ears, the feet, the hands and the nails. Use special foot care products and hand care products to keep these areas soft and gentle. Use cuticle products around the fingernail beds and the toenail beds. Utilize your choice of deodorants and perfume. Keep in mind to give yourself ample time for bathing and cleanliness. Special time is needed for the gently upkeep of your female body.   Enjoy this personal time and use the products that make you feel good.

Wear clean underwear every time that you have cleansed yourself. Be certain that panties are washed thoroughly with adequate soap, water, and fabric softener. Be sure that panties are not too tight and that they have cotton lining at the vaginal area to help prevent infection. New panties should be bought as often as you buy a new toothbrush: every three to six months. Old underwear carries old odors and do not benefit your hygiene. Your panties should be clean and fresh and your body should also be clean and fresh. Be equipped to handle discharges quickly to decrease body odor. Good sanitary habits and good hygiene will help to keep you healthy, looking good, and feeling wonderful.

In the space provided, list at least five most important characteristics that you want your mate to possess.

In the space provided, list at least five positive characteristics of your mate and compare them with the characteristics that you listed before.

List some positive reinforcement techniques and make note of those that empower your mate. Use these to encourage the positive characteristics that your mate already has and the positive characteristics that you want him to possess.

Notes

7 How To Keep Your Woman

Increased infidelity and the spiraling divorce rate in our great nation are clear indications that the relationship between men and women is in serious trouble. For this reason our families suffer greatly, and boys and girls are being raised without men, without male mentors, and without fathers. Therefore, men must learn that they are needed in all of our children's lives and that we need healthy men building healthy relationships with women. Sadly, too many relationships between men and women have only cushioned some men, not allowing them the opportunity to work hard in maintaining good relationships with women. Therefore much of society has resorted to infidelity and to just having sex. This action shows that many men and women have given up on marriage and monogamy and have yielded to infidelity and adultery.

When a man or woman has become adulterous, he or she has failed themselves and their mate. He or she must stop and repent instead of repeating the cycle. We must go back to the basics and teach men the importance of maintaining the responsibility in keeping one woman at a given time. When a man keeps one woman properly there is no time, no space, no money nor energy left to keep another woman. One woman is enough for one man if he is doing his part in the relationship. However, a man must first have the desire within himself to be monogamous and to have a healthy relationship.

First of all, keeping a healthy relationship with a woman should be a man's desire and it should be viewed by society as a manly thing to do. Playing the field, being unfaithful and untrustworthy, is the insecure and the childish thing to do and should be viewed by society as such. Before a man approaches a woman for dating, he should have considered the elements of having a healthy relationship. He should have already created and established the desire for a healthy relationship: companionship, commitment, and the search for a lifetime partner.

A man needs to examine himself and prepare himself spiritually,

48

socially, and physically in order to create the right desires for a healthy and permanent relationship with a woman. This endeavor needs to be done throughout his lifetime. Most importantly, a man's desire should not be so rampant and so out of control that he sees all women as sex objects. It is his responsibility to control his own unlawful desires. It is also his responsibility to create the right attitude where he views women as the wonderful work of God, one man each for every woman. A man who is on the loose may seek violation of another man's wonderful mate. While it is not good for man to be alone, it is even worse for man to violate another man's soul mate, when he could have his own wonderful soul mate.

When a man creates the right desire within himself for a woman, then he is responsible for seeking his soul mate who will share his goals and his honest desires for a healthy relationship. When a man is seeking to find his soul mate it does not give him license to use and to go through as many women sexually as he can. On the other hand this merely means that the man should analyze, assess, mentally evaluate and should be selective to find that special woman for himself. A man should have a great desire to keep a woman in a relationship. Keeping a woman means doing things that are important to her and doing some things that are unimportant to him. It also means doing the unselfish things that are needed for a healthy relationship.

A man should desire marriage and monogamy and should enjoy the work that is required in a relationship. His desire should only be toward his woman. If this is not the case, all other unlawful desires need to be modified by reading, counseling, praying, love, and exercising self control so that he can demonstrate the ability to keep a woman. The ability to keep a woman involves great communication skills and thoughtful attention to the woman.

Some men make a common mistake and get relaxed once they get the woman's attention. They start behaving as though the relationship is ready-made. The relationship is never ready-made because a relationship only stays connected through continued communication. During communicating the man should share his inner person, which is what he feels inside. He does this by sometimes sharing the events in his day. He also can do this by showing interest in the woman and asking about the events in her day.

He must practice these behaviors on an on-going basis. A man must learn to move beyond his desire to be silent and learn to reach out and share good conversation with the woman. He must practice communicating until it becomes his skill and also becomes enjoyable to him. He must learn to activate thoughtful and meaningful conversations with the woman. This means that his conversations should be about topics that are important to her and the relationship and not just about him and sports. While some women love sports and do enjoy this topic of conversation, men shouldn't get carried away on this subject!

Include social events, travel, spiritual and various other subjects in your communication. A man should never settle for appearing deaf, dumb, and blind to everything except when it comes to having sex. He should allow his senses to be alert to the woman and her concerns. However, in all that he does, he should be balanced. Don't talk too much, but also listen and pay attention to her signals. Be mindful that communication involves many things such as talking, listening, observing, hugging and a friendly kiss without tagging sex on to the kiss; back and neck massages, feet and hand massages without sex; giving roses and gifts without expecting sex. It also involves fulfilling the various likes and requests that the woman verbalizes. Add these and many more to your verbal and non-verbal communication. However, delete and avoid negative non-verbal communication.

The roaming eye is negative nonverbal communication that must be stopped. For example, a man may be on a date with one woman while watching another woman or watching every woman in his view. This action is disrespectful and it gives the nonverbal communication that this man is lustful and that he is a cheater. It also gives the nonverbal communication that this man is unappreciative of the woman he is dating, and that he is out of control. Some men even attempt to approve this action with a useless explanation. When a man acts in this manner, it doesn't matter what his explanation may be; this act is hurtful nonverbal communication.

While he is peeking and glancing at anything and everything in his view he should remember that he can't have what he is looking at, that moment. He must know at least that at this moment he is losing the one he is dating. He is losing her trust, her respect, her interest, her attention, and also he is losing the time that she wanted to spend with him. He may end up losing the relationship just for a cheap eye-full. Be sensible and realize that no one wants to go out with or be with a man who is always looking at something else or who is obviously looking for something else.

Some men even act as if they don't know that their eyes are roaming, while some do it and don't care. However, a man can stop this 'cold turkey.' He can start communicating positively to his mate. A woman can communicate more easily with a man who has integrity and a man who is hard working. Working is an old tradition that must fit into every generation, and men must work outside of the home as well as inside of the home. Keeping your woman means to preserve her. Some women work continuously, while they are at work and after they come home from work.

On the other hand, some men go to work and come home to watch the woman work as he relaxes by reading the newspaper or by watching TV. This is unfair. The man must show that he cares for the woman by helping her out around the house and with whatever else is needed. The relationship will work better when the man is a full participator, contributor, and supporter in the relationship. Also it wears on a woman's patience to always have to ask a man or remind him to help her work. In many ways a man can preserve the woman by doing what needs to be done and not waiting to be asked or to be told what to do.

Don't wait for her to have a heart attack by working too hard, but suggest that you help her and begin doing it. Don't do a little work and then sit down and let her finish the rest of the work, but sit down only when she is able to sit down. Get out of the habit of just preserving yourself but also preserve your mate so that she will be with you for a long time. This kind of effort to preserve your mate may also enhance the way that she views you as her man.

Physical appearance sometimes is one of the first things that bring about attraction to the opposite sex. Women are also interested in a man who takes good care of his health and his physical body. A man should have conquered foot odor and should have found a way to manage his personal hygiene before dating. Problems such as halitosis should be managed by flossing the teeth after meals and by brushing the teeth correctly. Men also should visit a dentist to learn about mouth care and should do this on a continuing basis. Also, he should wash his hair often and even use a dandruff shampoo if necessary.

Men, observe your weight as well; attend a gym or do some kind of weight lifting workout at home. Be an example and an encouragement to your mate in these areas. Take the leading role and monitor your own physical appearance. Today's women are not just accepting any man that comes along. Many are seeking their equal or someone who can uplift and encourage them in these areas. If you are a man who is not taking these measures, begin some of them immediately. Empower yourself to enhance your appearance.

Men! Don't lag behind women in the hygiene department but keep yourself physically fit and clean for the duration of the relationship. Consider, and manage your problems well. Most women don't mind having men who have problems, but they resent men who don't have solutions or don't know how to seek solutions to their problems. Also imperative in this discussion on physical appearance and personal hygiene is the flatus and passing gas that some men do without discretion. No woman want to be sitting down relaxing only to be surprised by a man's sudden burst of noise and a foul odor to follow. Remember that the bathroom is created for this purpose; be considerate and use the bathroom at these times. Also, it is not reasonable for a man to have poor hygiene and to have poor manners at home and expect for a woman to tolerate it. Be comfortable in your home and relax, but be considerate if you do not live alone.

Be balanced and use good discretion. Use the bathroom and the mirror appropriately but not obsessively. However, washing personal body parts such as the penis, scrotum, buttocks and underarms are vital. Wash the penis properly and adequately by pulling back on the foreskin of the penis and wash every area, lift up the scrotum and wash every area with a washcloth, soap and warm water. In the same way that men like for women to be clean, women also like clean men. Men must prepare for sex. Improve the relationship and don't just expect for sex to happen when you are repulsive because you are not clean.

Sex is an important part of keeping your woman. Being a clean and considerate man makes you more enticing to your mate for her to have sex with you. However, sex has been an area where men and women have not always found common ground. We must keep common ground in this area by communication, and both women and men must be honest about their likes and their dislikes. That which is pleasurable to one woman may be very unpleasant to the next woman. Therefore, a man is not a professional at sex simply because he was able to satisfy his last mate. I believe that a man must learn to be patient and not hasty about sex.

I hope that patience in this area will have come with reading and practicing patience all of the time. Patience is very important. The sexual climax is already very short, which is even more reason not to rush. This may entail practice and hard work at being patient, but men miss a lot of emotions because they rush. Patience will help men to take the time to hug, touch, caress and to engage in foreplay, instead of always jumping on the woman for a quickie and then jumping off her and go to sleep. When a man is patient, chances are that he will get quality sex and possibly get it more often. Men must elevate their minds and know the difference between sex and quality sex. In many cases a woman with the responsibility of family, work, and the household would prefer to have quality sex to having quantity sex. Men must take their time and perform sex patiently and well.

Handle your mate's body with care, passion, love, and not abusively. Limit your sexual activities to those that are acceptable and enjoyable to your mate and don't just expect your mate to be like the women that you have seen on the videos made for entertainment. Use safe and acceptable methods to develop, enrich, and excite your sexual activities without being offensive. With each sexual encounter create a special and wonderful sexual experience with your mate. Good sex just doesn't happen with a bang; it may take time to explore with your partner. If you want more of it, remember that sex is an unselfish act. A woman is more likely to have sex more often if the man is patient, unselfish, caring, loving, and if he performs well.

When premenstrual syndrome or menopause appears, be understanding instead of using this as an excuse for adultery or infidelity. Some women have found some relief for premenstrual syndrome and menopause while others continue to suffer with cravings, bloating, mood swings, headache, fatigue, sleeping a lot, irritability, weight gain or weight loss, and many other symptoms. If you are a strong man who has love, let your love be demonstrated also during these difficult times. Hormonal changes during these times are real and powerful, and these hormones sometimes overpower the woman's attitude and actions. Of course, if any woman is having severe symptoms, she must seek a physician's care. Don't allow PMS or menopause to ruin your relationship.

In this chapter are just a few tips to help men keep their women. Continue to read other books for more information. I encourage all men to find the desire and the passion again and take good care of their relationship. Take the responsibility to ensure that you are continuously involved in keeping a healthy relationship and that you are making the best possible relationship for your mate and for yourself.

HERE ARE SOME NICE THINGS TO DO TO HELP YOU KEEP YOUR WOMAN.

Pick a day out of the week when you will do the cooking, serve the table, feed the children, and wash the dishes.

Pick another day out of the week when you will give your mate a good neck and foot massage.

Pick a weekend out of the month when you allow your mate to sleep in and sleep late by herself with no bother from the phone, children, etc.

Make or buy your mate a personal gift, something that she needs.

Write a letter to your mate telling her why you are with her and why she is special.

Sit down, look your mate in the eye and ask her if she is happy.

Discuss your relationship and ways that you can improve it.

Be dedicated to having the best relationship possible with your mate and take responsibility for a better relationship.

SHIRLEY ROSE JONES

Notes

8 STRESS MANAGEMENT SKILLS THAT WILL CHANGE YOUR LIFE

Stress can go unrecognized by many individuals for long periods of time, but under these circumstances its influence on our body causes major problems. Some of the effects of stress eventually lead to the causes of death. Therefore, stress is in the same category of major diseases such as heart disease and cancer. We are not born with stress, and stress is not hereditary. The cure for stress is easy to achieve because it entails adopting a less stressful lifestyle. On the other hand, if we do not change our lifestyle, too much stress can cause serious illnesses. Therefore, "Stress Management Skills" should be a priority for us and should be at the top of everyone's list of concerns.

Everyone must become informed about stress in order to manage it. We must know that stress is when the major systems of our body are affected by life's difficulties and these systems become overwhelmed. When we think of stress, we identify it only with major crises such as unemployment, divorce or death, but it is the everyday stresses that we encounter that are most harmful to us. They are the immediate stress that we need to manage.

For example, Mr. Brown, a sales representative for a large corporation, had held his position for ten years. He was paid by commission and was so skilled that he was able to reach all sales demands on any given day. The main secretary of the corporation was ill and there was no secretarial replacement for her. On a cool spring day Mr. Brown went to work early because he was in such a pleasant mood and he wanted to start his day feeling good. Mr. Brown opened his office as he heard his phone ringing, and when he answered it the boss was calling, asking him to come to the front desk. He went with a big, bright smile, but suddenly his smile disappeared.

His boss asked him to work as the secretary for the day. Mr. Brown sat at the secretary's desk but he didn't know where to begin. He became very angry and frustrated, and he argued with everyone with whom he came in contact. At the later part of the day Mr. Brown was unable to meet the necessary typing deadline because his typing skills were inadequate. He received negative reports about his telephone etiquette and he did not keep good data on all of the telephone messages. Furthermore, he was very concerned about his sales position since his sale demands were not met that day.

At 5:30 p.m. Mr. Brown called home and informed his wife that he wouldn't be home at 6:00 p.m. for the special candlelight dinner that she had prepared for his birthday. Mrs. Brown responded, "I don't understand." "You always get home on time," and she slammed the phone down. Mr. Brown stayed at work until midnight in an attempt to organize the mess that he had created in the secretary's office. Due to enormous stress, he had skipped lunch and dinner and kept himself going with black coffee throughout the day and into the evening.

When Mr. Brown came home his wife was gone and he was unable to fall asleep because he had consumed too much caffeine that day. Early in the morning, at 2:00 a.m., when Mrs. Brown came home there was another argument. The next morning came too quickly for Mr. Brown. He was very tired when he arrived at work that morning. However, his boss asked him to work as the secretary indefinitely since the permanent secretary had to have major surgery and was uncertain when she would be able to return to work. He reluctantly accepted the challenge. But, if Mr. Brown handled the position the way he did the first day, even a vacation every three months wouldn't help him to cope with his problems. Mr. Brown must learn stress management skills so that he can control his reactions to daily activities and unexpected situations. He must learn how to use stress management skills to solve his daily problems.

Since everyone has stress; we accept stress as normal. We feel that we have no control over stress. However, you have lost control if you are not eating nutritiously and exercising regularly, if you do not have peace, joy and harmony, or if your job is not pleasing to you, if your needs for love and affection are not met by socializing with acquaintances, family and friends, or if there is no spirituality in your life and you are not aware of your feelings--then you need to begin to prioritize and to make gradual changes in your life. Until we make the important things a priority and organize our lives, we will always have lots of stress.

We are stressed because we place our health and our personal issues last on a daily basis and we allow our jobs and outside pressures to control our day. Also, we adapt to daily pressures without thinking and we don't even realize that these pressures consume us. Some of us even adjust to the concept that we must work under pressure; and many who don't assume this have still adapted to doing it. However, pressure equates to stress, and no one needs stress or pressure to achieve a task. This assumption that it takes some kind of pressure to make us do our best is untrue. Pressure causes nervousness and fear of failure. When any job is finished under these conditions, it gives a false sense of accomplishment but a true feeling of tiredness and stress.

If you are the type who does not finish a job unless someone pressures you, then you can learn to take responsibility for your discipline and you can motivate yourself in several ways. Become motivated by finding something enjoyable about the project that you are doing. Then set a time and a particular place for that project, as though this project is special and requires someone special like you to work on it. Give yourself a personal deadline and prioritize concerning the things that you need to do; don't work too hard or too long, but focus on the job that you are doing. Use pressure-relieving mechanisms such as fifteen-minute breaks. Try flexing and stretches for relaxation. Comfort and relaxation must be present in order to decrease stress and pressure. Sometimes it is even necessary to take a walk or to change position to relieve stress or pressure.

The pressures that we get from a boss or others on the job are also a major problem for many of us. Some employees accept these pressures in order to keep their jobs, and they therefore become completely stressed-out. They think that keeping the job is more important than decreasing stress, and they have a valid concern. How can we deal with such an unbearable boss? First, look at and examine the situation and realize that these types of supervisors have issues and they are unaware of stress management skills. However, an employee should not allow the situation to increase their stress. Instead, suggest that your corporation invest in a stress management skills class or seminar for all employees.

In the presence of a difficult supervisor or boss you can practice techniques such as breathing from the abdomen instead of breathing from the chest. Think of something pleasant; hold these pleasant thoughts for a while, then get back to work. Find someone to confide in and to talk to about these pressures. When talking about these pressures, let them go. Don't continue to dwell on them but release them, let them go and move on to the next discussion. Have a favorite family picture present to look at and to calm you during times of stress.

If your boss refuses to become informed about stress management skills then you have no other recourse but to keep your guard up when they are around you and to do this without feeling stressed. It is healthy to keep your distance from greatly frustrated people such as unbearable bosses who won't take the responsibility to help themselves and stop projecting their stress on to other employees. Also, on a daily basis find a pleasant area on the job away from your frustrated boss where you can relax for a moment. Seek ways to avoid confrontations with a mean or difficult boss, but by no means should you accept large amounts of stress from anyone.

Respond to any demeaning situation that a frustrated boss creates in a manner both wise and timely, but don't allow such situations to go unanswered because they will only get worse. Bosses are people too, and they have much vulnerability that can be pointed out and handled. They can be emotionally touched; however, your first concern is to love and to care for yourself. It is not beneficial to concentrate on ways to get back at your boss, but it is beneficial to create a plan on what to do in order to demand respect from everyone around you including a difficult boss.

Be informed of the numerous signs and symptoms of stress. These signs and   symptoms can be more easily recognized when they are broken down into psychological, behavioral, and physical symptoms. The symptoms of stress can touch every organ and system of our bodies. The symptoms of stress can lead to severe illnesses such as heart disease, hypertension, cancer, ulcers, colitis, and many other major diseases. When stress is ignored and unmanaged, it gets to the stage of 'total exhaustion' or 'total burnout.' The individual feels hopeless, selfless, and out of control.

Therefore, it is important for us to be knowledgeable of the various signs and symptoms of stress so that professional help can be sought. Here are some of the signs and symptoms of stress that affect the psychological and mental processes. They are: poor judgment, forgetfulness, emotional exhaustion, inability to concentrate, inability to solve problems, difficulty processing information, inability to make decisions, insomnia, anxiety, anger, nervousness, nightmares, fear, moodiness.

Others symptoms, listed below, affect one's behavior and are referred to as behavioral symptoms. They are: argumentativeness, anorexia, absenteeism, overeating, accidents, bulimia, frequent urination, over-spending, vomiting, drug abuse, alcohol abuse, and withdrawal from friends. The final symptoms listed below affect the physical body and are referred to as physical symptoms, and they are: night sweats, headache, heart palpitation, constipation, neck pain, migraines, light-headedness, decreased sex drive, diarrhea, tension, amenorrhea, panic attack, chest pains, back pain and heartburn.

Managing stress requires that a person become aware of and takes responsibility for his or her own lifestyle or situation. Also, they must look at their health and their happiness and decide their first priority. Good health is emotional, physical, social and psychological balance. There must be an emphasis on each of these for your own happiness, thereby preparing you to get through the day with a minimum amount of stress no matter what happens. This means being conscious about stress: Think before reacting to any situation and then act in your own interest. Health and happiness are the ultimate goals for everyone's life, because without these two goal achievements we cannot be successful at anything else.

Learning to have a flexible temperament that will adjust to any changes gives you peace, optimum energy, and tolerance in your working relationships and in your family relationships. Therefore, having flexibility is one of the keys in managing stress. However, never allow flexibility to stop you from saying "no" when "no" is necessary. Also important in managing stress is taking time-out or a break when needed. Taking time-out or a break is not a waste of time. Instead time-out or a break improves energy which allows for more concentration to complete daily duties. Although all of these methods are vital, ultimately we must STOP, pay attention to our mind and our body, and relax. Also, bear in mind that we should be realistic in answering the two questions below to minimize stress: What really makes you happy? What is your life all about?

How an individual reacts to a situation determines if they have allowed the situation to become stressful. It is not always the situation alone, but it is often the reaction to the situation that makes the difference. For example, Mr. Davis and Mr. Johnson worked for the same company. They were both fired unexpectedly for no faults of their own. However, Mr. Davis was bitter, depressed and had intense anger. Meanwhile, Mr. Johnson took the firing as an opportunity to look at himself, to explore his creativity and to start his own business. The method Mr. Davis used for coping created stress while Mr. Johnson motivated himself and used a resourceful coping method. The manner in which we perceive and interpret circumstances determines whether we experience stress. The result of our reaction shows whether we used a positive coping method.

In any stressful situation, remember that mind over matter works. The mind controls the body and the reaction since the important transmitters of the brain are affected immediately as stress appears. The cortex of the brain transmits information from the environment to the brain. This cortex processes understanding, processes problem solving, and processes decision-making. Also, the cortex transmits communication with the limbic system, which is the emotion-control area. Therefore, the limbic system, which consists of the nerves and the hormones, is connected to the thought area.

Obviously, practicing thought control is another way to manage stress. For example, think about how you reacted when you were stuck in a traffic jam that made you late for work. What were your immediate reactions and your first thoughts? The best way to deal with a traffic jam is to control your thinking. Do this by not dwelling on the thought that you will be late for wherever you are going. Instead, be positive and consider the traffic jam to be the ideal time to pause, take a break, and resourcefully think of something appropriate to do, all the while keeping your eyes on the road.

Getting stressed will not change the traffic jam. Therefore, change and control that which you have the power and the will to change and control: your thinking. Your mind can control your emotions. The type of personality you have also helps to determine your capacity in managing stress. For instance, the type "A" personality has a more difficult time with stress. However the same concept applies, because mental processes do control personality. The major part of personality is learned behavior. Personality can be adapted by the willingness to apply and to practice new learning as your knowledge increases.

Another skill that minimizes stress is good breathing techniques. Most of us breathe incorrectly from our chest. Due to this incorrect breathing pattern most of us are practicing stressful breathing throughout the day. In this case, when we encounter stress we breathe fast and we inhale a smaller amount of air. However, healthy breathing is when we breathe from the abdomen evenly and with slower breaths. This breathing technique allows much more air into the lungs, which gives more oxygen to the blood stream. It also causes the heart to pump more easily and gives more adequate nourishment to the body's cells. This breathing pattern decreases the respiratory and the heart rate, and this sends signals to the brain to become aware that there is no danger. Thus, abdominal breathing should be practiced immediately in any uncomfortable situation since it causes all of the body's systems to return to the resting state and not the alarm state. Even the muscles begin to relax.

We women must now wonder how we can apply stress management skills to the children and the household. The reality is that it is possible to live with children regardless of their age, and to have less stress. One of the most important methods in this is organization and awareness. We must develop a system that works and benefits all parties involved and we must recognize when we are about to become stressed. If stress goes unnoticed it will increase, and eventually it will overwhelm the person. Therefore, we cannot just ignore the signals of stress.

Let us begin a dialogue about organization, which can be described as a system that is consciously and repeatedly used to achieve a goal. Let's talk about those of us who have concluded that we are just not organized. We all have heard someone say, "I am just not organized." However, when an individual has made up their mind that certain things have a particular place and that some things can be done better a certain way, their lives are less stressful. I don't mean that a person has to be 'obsessive' about order.

I simply mean that a person must be organized enough to keep their lives on a regular schedule. Any system, if repeatedly used, will become 'second nature.' Therefore, if a person constantly practices being unorganized, it will be 'second nature' to them, but if they work on a system of order, this also will become natural to them. However, the challenge at first is to plan a system, initiate it, and make a conscious effort to use it. Although at first it may seem that it's not working or that nobody is following it, continue your efforts. Your goal is to implement a plan and to follow it. Eventually it will catch on and become a part of your life.

Another part of organization is learning how to delegate responsibility. Women, don't assume all of the workload. Find something that everyone can do to help you at home. For example, if you go to the store and buy two bags of groceries, don't carry both of them because they are light. Give one to your son or to the person who may be walking beside you and let them help you. Get everyone in the habit of doing something around the house. Well, one might say, I will just do it myself instead of taking the energy to ask for help. However, we must forsake this myth and delegate responsibility to those who are capable. Be serious about not being a slave in your own home. Encourage everyone to work together and to have fun together. Use your brainpower to plan a system that involves everyone.

Since the house never stays clean because of microbes and dust all around, try cleaning one room at a time. Instead of doing everything the same day, do the laundry one day of the week and the cleaning on another day. Do the house cleaning on a day when everyone is home. Allow someone to do the furniture, someone to do one bathroom and someone to do the refrigerator, etc. Express gratitude and allow each one to take responsibility to clean up their mess. Women, we must remember to share the work and that we can't do it all. However, be consistent in whatever plan you decide to use.

Children sometimes need good disciplinary action when you don't have the energy to discipline. Many times 'go to your room' is just what they want to hear. A good method is to have them write about the matter for which they are being punished. Other punishments for older children can include chores such as ironing and cleaning the house. These kinds of punishments will make them mindful of cleanliness and will help you at the same time.

One good idea is to have a time set aside for you. Call it "mommy's time," and let everyone in the house know not to disturb you during this time unless there is an emergency. Give the baby to your husband or let your sister or friend come over for a couple of hours to watch the baby while you take *your* time. Relax and do something for yourself, or do something that you love doing. Your children will grow up respecting your time of peace and not just expecting you to ignore yourself and always do for them. If you have older children, let them know that you need your space and don't let neighbors or friends infringe on this time unless it is urgent. This time and space, every day, will allow you to recuperate and replenish. It will allow you to let your guard down and just enjoy a little freedom. The double impact of work will hit you hard if you don't know how and when to get away from them.

Although women have too many ways for stress to enter their lives, they also have the advantage of having the outlets to release these stresses. Regardless of how many bills you have, put a few dollars on the side and call it the "good time" fund. Treat yourself by going to the beauty salon, spa, or out to dinner once a month or as often as you can afford a treat. However, be dedicated to this fund. Treat yourself. Make the time and the effort to enjoy you, and have a great time without rushing home. Be wise and don't overdo it, but take ample time to enjoy yourself.

Also, find a hobby or something that you enjoy doing which doesn't cost you any money. Resort to it if and when you don't have the money to spend. If we will give ourselves a little attention, people will respect us and give us a little more of their love and attention to add to what we have given ourselves. On the other hand, if they see us treating ourselves harshly or allowing everyone else to have a good time but us, then they will adapt to that same habit. You do not always need your husband or friend to initiate being good to you, because you can learn to be good to yourself, and perhaps they will join this habit. Show yourself a good time by joining an exercise group, setting appointments for a massage, cooking something special for yourself, getting a pedicure, and so on. There are so many outlets for us women to use to get rid of stress if we take the time to do it.

Having good friends will improve your success in managing stress. Good friends are those who will be glad to help you get your life in order. Those who insist that you remain everyone's footstool are not good friends. Seek as friends people who have a good attitude towards life. Avoid stressful relationships with friends since you will have enough stress at home. If you have a long-time friend who causes stress in your life and you don't want to give up that friendship, then take the responsibility to guide the conversations and give her books to read with a positive outlook on life. Discuss the book in your conversations, and make the discussion enjoyable. None of us should allow someone to drag us down into his or her struggles. If we are not able to bring a negative person up to positivity then we are forced to consider other options, since our primary purpose on this earth is not to work hard and to die but to live a healthy and a happy life.

In conclusion, let's practice some skills that help to manage stress: First, recognize the stress in your daily life. Avoid encountering stress. Reducing exposure to any kind of stress will help, because the objective is to establish a balance between the negative and the positive forces. Second study yourself, your personality type and your usual ways of dealing with situations. You can help yourself if you search within yourself for answers concerning your coping style and personality. Third, invest in proven learning skills, such as relaxation techniques and prayer.

List the names of people, by initials that promote stress in your life.

You can list methods to decrease the stress from these people.

Find ten quick stretches that immediately cause 'de-stressing'. Remember these and do them when stress is upon you.

List pleasant hobbies you can do to 'de-stress' you.

Make time every day to get rid of tension and stress build-up.

Write down the time of day that you will do the things in your life that 'de-stress' you and make a commitment to do them.

Take the time every day for pleasure reading.

A worksheet is provided to make the list requested above and to write down anything else that you desire. Please utilize this worksheet.

SHIRLEY ROSE JONES

Worksheet

Notes

9 YOU ARE SPECIAL

When you accentuate your positive characteristics with grace and without pomposity, you allow yourself and the world to see and appreciate them. It helps you to feel healthier and happier when these, the best parts of you, emerge in a continuous manner. God created you unique and special. Therefore, remember; you are always unique and special in every way and on every day.

The color of your skin doesn't matter, neither does it matter how you look on the outside. It doesn't matter if you are overweight or underweight, if you were abused or if you had bad childhood experiences. You are indeed special in the world, and you belong here. It doesn't matter how hard life has been for you, or how poor you may have been; you are special and the world needs a special person like you in it. Your name may not be as elaborate as a movie star's name. You may even be struggling and unable to see anything special about yourself.

Even if you can't see it now, it is imperative that you know and understand that everything and everyone God created is significant and special, including you. God created you, and you have a special gift and talent to offer the world; you are not a mistake. You are an important human being in this vast world and you belong here with us. Therefore, view yourself as a distinguished person with your own unique qualities. There are many special gifts, talents, creativities and positive characteristics embedded within your soul and within your spirit that are unique to you. Acknowledge the best of yourself; give your best to yourself and to the world. The world is waiting on these characteristics. Search yourself for these characteristics. When you find out what they are, release them into the world.

It is with this great and deliberate release of your beautiful characteristics that you can feel yourself beginning to advance. People around you will see and they will feel a lifting like the taking off of an airplane. They will feel it also when you come completely into the knowledge that you are special and when this knowledge becomes a part of your conduct. As you come into this knowledge, low self-esteem leaves and a certain kind of freedom begins to happen. At this remarkable unfolding, you should not allow anything to stop you from completely evolving. During this time when the specialty in you explodes, let it explode; you are well on your way to evolving and you should not allow anything to turn you back.

Hard times, pain, low self-esteem and bad experiences can sometimes disguise your gift and your specialties. In order to help prevent this camouflaging, you might sit down and list ten things that are great and extraordinary about you. It will be beneficial to write these in large and bold letters to maximize them in your heart. Allow this to be an awakening but also a humbling experience.

Placing an explanation or an example beside each characteristic and the effect of these characteristics on your life and on the lives of others will encourage you to use the list more often. Family and friends can help you with this exercise if you are unable to list ten characteristics on your own. When you realize and accept these beautiful and special gifts that the world is waiting to enjoy, you will feel empowered and you can enjoy these special gifts yourself. You can then enjoy sharing them with the world.

For example, you may have on your list that you are a kind person. You may have as an explanation that when a stranger fell down the stairs you showed kindness. While everyone else laughed, you helped the stranger to his feet. The result may have been that the stranger smiled and said, "thank you very much." Use this same kindness that you used towards the stranger for yourself, and pick your own self up. Be kind to yourself always and enjoy your kindness. Since you may do exceptionally well in showing kindness, spread your kindness to those who need and appreciate it. There are plenty of people in this world who need a kind word to survive the day. It is so spectacular to know that a person does not have to have a dime in their pockets, but they can change somebody's life through kindness. Emphasizing and utilizing your talent in times of need will change you and others in a significant way. It will also help you to focus and to cultivate these characteristics, which allows your talent to mature. Continue to release your talent into the world. Spreading your talent with confidence and humility in the world empowers you and other people around you.

These positive characteristics when they are released can also be used to overcome obstacles that are in your life. Tragedies, misfortunes, and difficult experiences are a part of everyone's life. These will also come into your life. When obstacles and difficult circumstances face you, emphasize your positive characteristics and your talent. Consciously verbalize, emphasize and utilize all of the characteristics that you have listed. Use them to handle any unfortunate situation. Ignoring or denying any difficult situations will not be effective, but using your specialty and positive characteristics will help you to overcome difficulties. Working hard at using your specialties will make the difference during difficulties.

Social environmental hazards can also hinder your specialties, but you can also overcome these hazards. It is true that selecting and choosing to surround yourself with positive people will help your specialty to grow. Associating with people who appreciate you makes it easier to release your specialties. On the other hand, bad and negative associations can place a damper on your goal which is to spread your talent in the world. There are those who you may consider family and friends who will want to rely upon your talent. They will desire to keep their talent for themselves while using yours. Some of these people may view you as weak when you use your specialty. They may even try to manipulate you. Be encouraged to insist by your actions and verbalizations that their gifts and talents are worth sharing. Insist that they share their specialty with you and the world for enlightenment and enjoyment. It is a good thing to learn about other people's talent and to allow them to learn about yours.

When you embark upon people who have empowered themselves, you should permit their specialness to administer to you in whatever way necessary. It is advantageous to observe other's gifts and to make them aware of their own gifts. It is also advantageous to promote others and to encourage them to practice their specialty. This benefits you and them at the same time. On the other hand, it is a disadvantage to conceal other people's gift from them or to be jealous of the success of their gift. It is rewarding to feel thankful and gracious and to cherish the specialness of others.

Your talent will be more productive if you insist that others treat your talent with respect. Appreciating your specialties and the specialness of others creates the space and the atmosphere for goodness and blessings. This appreciation also establishes an environment for further talent to develop. These principles direct your focus on positive characteristics. You therefore become more attractive or drawn to people who have their specialness exposed and who are affecting this world positively. These principles, when applied, make it easier for you to gravitate toward the final entrance of a refreshed self-esteem and the throwing-off of the weight of the feeling of insignificance.

As you move more strongly into your positive characteristics, you must also move very strongly out of bad habits, the feeling of insignificance, negativity, and any other characteristic that hinders your talent. You must shed these and let them go forever. You may list the things that hinder your talent in small letters. You may minimize them by writing them in pencil. Every time these hindrances confront you, use your power to conquer them. You must encourage yourself to acknowledge these hindrances, and use prayer to help you overcome them. When you give in to these hindrances it strengthens them; therefore never give in to them. We must all still love the positive and negative about ourselves, but come out of the negative and live more strongly in the positive. We must protect our specialness from those who are jealous or who try to block us from our best selves. Part of our purpose is to use our specialty and radiate the world and to always shine bright.

Some people are filled with darkness and they refuse to accept light. They have the right to choose darkness over light. However, we must be able to spot these people and not allow them to block or to hinder our brightness. We must love that which God has made special about us. We must learn how to use it effectively and purposefully. Share it with the world wisely to make life rich and flavorful. Give God praises for making you special and ask Him how to use these special qualities to fulfill your destiny in your lifetime.

Important Self-Evaluation

List the characteristics that make you unique and demonstrate the ways in which you enhance people's life.

Name the things that you can do to make the world a better place.

Name the things that you are going to start doing today to make the world better.

How can you make a difference in everything that you do?

Name your special touch. Do you make people smile, feel comfortable etc. with this special touch?

WORKSHEET

Complete your evaluation on this page and you may ask yourself any other questions that may help you to recognize your specialties. Be certain to completely answer any questions that you develop.

10 TIME

To everything there is a season, and a time to every purpose under the heavens: A time to be born and a time to die; A time to plant, and a time to pluck up that which is planted; A time to kill, and a time to heal; a time to break down, and a time to build up; A time to weep, and a time to laugh; A time to mourn, and a time to dance, A time to cast away stones, and a time to gather stones together; A time to embrace, and a time to refrain from embracing; A time to get, and a time to lose; A time to keep and a time to cast away: A time to rend, and a time to sew; A time to keep silence, and a time to speak; A time to love, and a time to hate; A time of war, and a time of peace. (Ecclesiastes 3: 1- 8) King James Version.

In this chapter, being on time is being where you should be divinely. This means being on schedule with the exact blueprint that God has for your life. It is accepting the exact blueprint, the plan that was ordained for you, and giving this plan the development needed to make this plan happen and to make this plan work. It is being age-appropriate and not allowing yourself to become late or behind in the years given to you to fully complete your plan. Completing your plan is essential to completing your purpose in life. Therefore, the moment is appropriate for you to evolve and to abide by the divine plan for your life. Most of us are guilty of sometimes being off track   or even running in the opposite direction and going against the plan for our life.

Now is the moment to get back to the plan for your life. Begin where you left off in doing those tasks that must be finished and contribute to the order for the divine plan for your life. Now is the moment of realization to get back to the things that really matter. Come into and remain into your individual moment no matter what is going on. When you are in your moment, which is your exact plan and blue- print, it is impossible for you to get too busy doing other things.

Also, when you are where you are supposed to be in life you have harmony with yourself and with your soul. It takes away the stress and unimportant things from your life. Doing what you are called to do every day and moving on course with your time given to you is peace. This kind of timing takes minute-by-minute concentration and focusing. When you surrender to the original plan for your life and don't become distracted or moved out of place, then you are on time. This kind of lifestyle gives you rest and harmonize your life.

While we know that we must harmonize our lives, unfortunately many of us continue to miss-time our lives. We do this by being lazy and by being undisciplined. We become unaware of the things that we need to do and we just let go of our lives. When we are not on schedule for our lives we miss-time everything that is important for our productivity. We go down a path where everything is off balance and out of place. It also becomes difficult to regain the time that we lose. When this happens to us we must recognize it and change the unproductive direction in which we are heading.

We must come to a complete stop, turn around and begin to take the steps necessary to turn our lives into the direction of our individual moment. This can be done and it must be done. For us to do anything successfully we must understand when the moment is exact and appropriate. I call this coming of age and synchronizing with time.

This does not indicate that a person has to be forty years old to be synchronized in their timing. Although it has taken many people forty years to acknowledge time, it does not have to be so for you. You can enjoy your life's journey in a timely manner that is set at an early age. When you start early to evolve in your personal moment you will avoid many mistakes, bad experiences and devastating downfalls. This requires that instead of following friends and associates you should continue to do the things that must be done in your own life. For example, young people who continue to make good grades in school must continue to feed their minds, souls and bodies only things that are good for them and they must delete all untimely people out of their lives.

Young people can keep their lives on track into adulthood. If the youthful generation has missed-time, they must just move their lives back into their individual moment. Young people can control almost everything that happens in their lives if they dismiss the things that are not in their momentum and accept those things that are in their time and synchronization. When the youth of today is doing all things well and something bad or opposing comes along, they should reject it strongly. Accept the offers that add to the good that you are doing and move in your moment that is given to you. When you are in the moment for your life you have the power to reject opposition.

Many famous people have made many great discoveries in their time, but each person must make their own personal discoveries. The first discovery that an individual must make personally in his time is that each person must know who God is, and live according to God's Word. After a person has done this, the work begins. This work is that each person has the job of discovering who he or she is within and without in the appropriate time.

We spend many years in school studying and becoming fascinated by the major discoveries that others have made in their lifetimes. While this is very praiseworthy and is very important, most of these discoverers never discovered themselves. Many of us follow the same pattern of achieving and doing great work and we will never discover or know our moment or ourselves. When this happens it is easy to be unhappy or to even lose what we have gained. One of the most important discoveries is when we know without a shadow of a doubt what we are, and to whom we belong; this is our origin. This entails knowing all of the vital things about us and accepting them. This is our duty to ourselves and to mankind.

In order to evolve in your specific moment, you must know yourself. You must discover the greatness that God has given you and be thankful and accept this greatness. You must know who you are in the world and who you are meant to become in the world. While this is just the starting point, you must also know your negative emotions and your positive emotions, thereby protecting these emotions by not allowing people or trials and tribulations to manipulate these emotions.

You should have a good idea of the direction that you must go toward and follow. You must have a well-rounded knowledge of your own disposition in life and of the kind of people who are needed in your own life at any given time. At this juncture, timing is vital. In order to make a purposeful connection with others who can help to energize and to ignite your dream, you must be in a particular rhythm. You must be in the rhythm of knowing part of you, some of you, or most of you.

This rhythm will also help you to recognize the right kind of people. It will help you to recognize that many people are doing the right thing and are accepting the challenge of fulfilling their purpose. Who you are and what you were meant to do in this life must be one of your major lifetime discoveries. You should discover and know at a very early age how you will impact the world and your environment.

If you don't know this already, start now; begin your investigation of yourself and make this discovery. Do not become discouraged, instead become enthusiastic and determined. Being born a baby girl or a baby boy was just your entry into society. Each of us has a divine purpose in this world. No one is a waste or is no-good. There is good inside all of us. It is up to us to discover what that good is and how we must use our good to help to correct wrong in our lives, the lives of others, and the rest of the world.

Although you may have done everything wrong up until now, you can still make changes. If you are confused about yourself and you don't know where to begin, ask yourself or someone you trust to show you positive things about you. Find out how that good in you can help the world and the people around you. You must come to know your goodness and know how to show that goodness in society. Your goodness might be different from the goodness of others, but it is needed in society. You have not begun to meet yourself until you introduce your own goodness into your own life and then into the lives of others.

Some people live their entire life without knowing themselves. They look at themselves externally in the mirror daily, and they never see themselves internally for a moment. On the other hand, many others may see themselves but they deny what they see. They have wasted their lives doing bad things and doing evil things, and they thought that's who they were. They are mistaken because for their entire life they never got to know themselves or their goodness.

They have ignored, overlooked, and destroyed the beautiful characteristics that they were given to change their own lives and to also change the lives of others. They have committed lifetime suicide and they have wiped out a whole generation by killing the goodness that is in them, while still merely existing in this world. Don't let this happen to you. Come out of the confusion of not knowing by accepting who you are and the person that you were meant to be. Get rid of your negative conduct; empower and feed your goodness. Feed your goodness so that it will reproduce perpetually, constantly, and in a timely manner.

The major battle that we have in life is a battle within ourselves. This battle is eminent when we don't allow ourselves to be cultivated. Our war and our battles are not with others; they are with ourselves when we are not yielding to our change of moment. Whenever a moment for change was apparent and we ignored this moment to change, we engaged ourselves in dangerous and overwhelming battles. Many have died from heart attacks, strokes and hypertension fighting themselves; they refused to yield to the pain of self-discovery and self-growth.

Our will and everyday preoccupations stop us from yielding to our moment of change. We must be mindful that all stubborn wills must be broken and they must be retrained by us to be flexible. Begin by finding your goodness and operate it by refusing to give in or to yield to the demons of this world. Come into your momentum time of knowing you. Come into your moment of whom you are and where you are supposed to be in life.

Take the first move on the game board of life; you will win by being on time for your self-evolving. We are supposed to evolve every day and every moment. Time does not stop; it keeps on ticking. Your life does not stop; it keeps on moving with time. Even when you are asleep and you are resting, your heart and your life keep on moving, growing, and evolving with time. We cannot stop this   process   and we do not have the control to slow it down.

Therefore, we cannot waste time. We must get rid of the clutter in our space and in our human closets, thereby having this space to occupy our lifetime adequately. In other words, we must get our life on the path and on the course for doing the work, the job and all of the things that we were put on this planet to do. Whenever you fall short and you find yourself doing destructive things to yourself and to humanity, just STOP! Take a break and find the one good thing that you are able to do.

It doesn't matter how small it may be or how insignificant it may seem. It could be that you have a beautiful smile. Go about smiling and using your goodness positively. Be cautious not to allow anyone to misuse or misunderstand your smile, but use it positively and freely. It could also be that you have a beautiful voice; use it and sing. Use it in a good way, and be aware that you are using your goodness. You must begin somewhere, so begin enjoying and sharing your own goodness. Be happy about it, whatever it is, and let it help change you and connect you with yourself, your blueprint, and your path.

In order to make a smooth joining of your path and yourself you must first forgive yourself. Forgive yourself for waiting so long and wasting so many precious moments of your time going around in circles for so many years. Forgive yourself for allowing circumstances to push you around and out of your time zone. It could be that you passed your husband or wife-to-be on life's way, and missed your moment because you were full of pent up selfishness, insecurity, and un-forgiveness. Go back down the same road that you came up by giving up the selfishness, insecurity and un-forgiveness. You may be pleasantly surprised that gifts and blessings are just waiting there for you to come into your moment and to receive them. You must pass by those points in life and only accept and receive those wonderful gifts that are waiting for you as you come into your own moment.

Forgiveness is most often one of the important steps in the process of connecting within you. It is appropriate to forgive yourself and everyone else. It is appropriate to give up hate, malice, unloving thoughts and emotions, which simply means--forgive all. You can turn your moment around into the right direction by pushing the un-nourishing emotions and thoughts out and creating room for self-love and love for others to grow. When you let go of pent up emotions it is easier to open up to love and strength.

This enables us enormous speed and the ability to catch up on being in our moment for ourselves and utilizing the moment that's been given to us. The adverse is that an unforgiving spirit is a weak spirit and it causes mistrust toward others. There are no exceptions; it doesn't matter who it is or what others have done. Un-forgiveness aborts our time. You will never be in your correct time abiding with un-forgiveness.

An unforgiving heart is a burden, a hindrance, and it is death to your moment. No one can successfully achieve anything and keep it while holding on to un-forgiveness. You must let the un-forgiveness go in order to be in the moment for your life. Give back the harm that was given to you by gathering up everything toxic and handing it over to God, or just simply place it into the trash or into the dumpster. Do not hold on to even a minuscule situation. When you forgive you set the time clock for your life. Imagine your entire life without carrying the weight of un-forgiveness. Can you see how much more you will be able to accomplish and how much faster you will accomplish your life's task? You will meet your moment and your personal best if you put down un-forgiveness. The person or thing that you have not forgiven, are they worth you missing your moment. Of course not! Escape by forgiving, and run into your moment.

The quicker that you forgive the more you can achieve and the more time you have given yourself to achieve more things. Within your scope of time allotted to you in your life by God there is love, finding your soul mate, educational achievements, job advancement, and performing that which you were born to do in this world. You must forgive so that you are on time for these events in your life. It is well overdue for you to get your benefits in this life. Your reward in this world is waiting for you to get on the path of your life. Once you have scheduled your heart to discover and to use your divine time, your success will be consistent. After finishing one goal, there is another waiting. One accomplishment promotes another. One good thing creates another good thing. We must purposely set ourselves to be timely in our lives.

Also, it is greatly beneficial to us when we associate with peers who are time conscious. The remarkable truth is that when we are in the right place in our lives at the right time in our lives, we cannot be denied. The people around us in the outside world will know that it is our moment. Once we have practiced timing our objectivity, a process of connection will happen. Timing it, going for it, and getting it are the result of great determination. We must practice aiming, timing, and hitting the targets in life again and again.

Life is about becoming an expert on our timing, and us, and also becoming an expert on other people's timing. First we must have total knowledge and wisdom about what's in us; we must know this in order to be ready to seize the moment and the time. We must no longer allow the moment and the time to escape us. We must learn principles and actions that connect with our effort; we must aim perfectly for our perfect moments. Seek God's help and wisdom in relating to the optimum moment and knowing when the perfect time is come.

It's time to let the world know that you are here and that you are in this world to complete a job. Your timing is the opportunity that you have given yourself to begin and to complete life, while constantly doing that which you were placed here to do. During this process of connecting with your moment it is necessary to always remove everything that distracts you and gets in the way of your perfect timing. You must develop and practice tremendous respect for time. You must occupy and spend time wisely. When it's time to rest, exercise, or socialize you must do it accordingly, allowing the right thing to happen. It is your moment to recognize the essence of your life. Your time, well utilized, will make you millions of dollars and change the course of your life.

Apply time to what you do, and measure your time. Use time skillfully and make time work in your favor every moment of every day. When you lose count, immediately get back to count. Be on time in your life every day. Also, until sickness or death occurs, you have today and this moment to correct your errors. Don't delay in correction of your errors or mistakes. Do over what you are allowed to do over, and be on time in doing it. Try never to be a procrastinator or one who always delays. Make a relentless effort not to ignore the time to do today what you must do today.

It's time to change. At this moment, begin to change those things that slow you down. Change the things that you know are horrible about you and put yourself in the zone of your moment. Do this by saying what you mean to yourself and meaning what you say. For example, if it is needed, tell yourself "no." Say it, mean it, and stand behind it. No, I will not continue to lose and waste precious and valuable time. Your time to do something positive about your negatives is now. Get up. Stand up and make the changes. It Is Time.

HONEST REMINDERS

Be aware of your short-term goals by placing them on your daily calendar and reading them daily.

Keep a productive mind by placing your long-term goals in view. Write them on a calendar that you will look at every week.

Start the achievement process of reaching your goals today. Don't delay!

Use something to center and focus you by beginning your day with a form of discipline such as reading a scripture, listening to a certain song or doing certain exercises, etc.

Don't become distracted. Remove all distractions and remain focused.

Enjoy planning for your life and achieving goals. Don't make this process stressful, but make it fun and peaceful.

Notes

11 YOUR ASSOCIATES AND FRIENDS MATTER

Many of us have heard the phrase or the philosophy that association brings on assimilation. This phrase and philosophy bears some reality and some truth. It does make a difference who we spend most of our time talking to and being around, because we either adapt to their behaviors or they adapt to our behaviors. For this reason we do not want our children to be around gang members or to have any undisciplined friends. We encourage our children not to be involved with people who are in and out of jail or who do not respect authority. This is excellent advice, and our children should obey it. However, at this time let's guide ourselves by holding to the same philosophy. Also, let us now examine our own personal network of associates and friends. Let us start by knowing the difference between associates and friends.

Friends are special people who know our positive and our negative characteristics and love us despite these characteristics. Friends are in our lives for the purpose of enriching our lives and should never negatively influence us in any way. They are a stable and positive force, no matter how bad things get. Our friends will be our friends even if we do not have substance such as money to give to them in return for love or friendship. Friends will understand us and our personal situations when no one else does and will stand by us.

However, a true friend will not allow us to do wrongful things or allow us to let bad circumstances overtake us without attempting to help. A friend will be able to correct us when we are in error and will be able to help to direct us toward the right path. There is no place for jealously in a friendship because a friend always wants the best and the right situations for us. A friend will never let us down or lead us astray. A friend will be willing to apologize when they are wrong and will also be willing to accept our apologies. Friendship takes a lifetime to discover and a lifetime to establish. By all means, we should keep good friends and value them dearly.

On the other hand, some of us will begin to examine the people around us and realize that, in spite of all of the years invested in the relationship, some people are not true friends. Some of us will walk away from old relationships once we come to know that these people near and dear to us are not our friends. We will insist that our friends uphold positive standards or we will insist they separate themselves from us. We will begin to seek to enjoy a sincere, honest, positive and enriching relationship from a friend.

We will now distinguish between associates and friends and will maintain each in their respective places. An associate is a contact person whom we have met with or conversed with, but associate relationships are not intimate, having a strong bond. There may be many similarities and things to share with an associate, but there isn't enough information, shared experience or love to call this person a friend. Some associates become friends, but we must know when the change occurs and be certain that such change occurs on both sides of the relationship. Still, an associate should be a positive influence in our lives and should help to point our lives in the right direction.

In many instances some of us have had people in our lives that hold us back and prevent us from realizing our dreams. We must single them out one by one. Notice or remember all of the challenges in your life. Assess who caused these challenges and assess how your associates benefited you. If by singling out all of your associates you find those who influence you in doing the things in life that are not advantageous, you should release that bad associate or talk it over with them. You should be able to influence your associates positively and you should be strong enough to say no or yes when necessary.

We must be careful to get control of any negative associates or to release them, because negative associates can destroy our dreams, our goals, and our life. On the other hand, associates should be in our life to support and to encourage us to realize our creativity and to help us reach our destiny in life. There should be fun, growth, and progress in our group of associates whether this group is small or large. If we have found that throughout the years we have not accomplished our goals, we must examine what we do in our leisure time with our associates.

Motivation and the desire to meet our goals should first come from us and then secondly from our associates. Motivation is very important, and all of us must know ways to get ourselves in a motivated spirit. Being 'pumped up' and ready for our daily task is something that should always be present with us, or we should be able to obtain this through friends or associates. However, some of us meet conflicts and tremendously hard times, and we may find it difficult to remain motivated. If you are having a difficult time with motivation, examine your associates.

Some associates are not always good and do not always wish us well. Jealousy and envy are some of the difficulties that can be present within the circle of some associations. We must be careful to examine our associations and to be aware of jealously and envy. We must be encouraged to empower our associates with love and encouraging words. However, as we give love and uplifting words to our associates we must also receive the same from them.

We must be on the alert to stay away from bad associations. Bad associations will impede our progress and will keep us entangled in doing wrong. People who insist on not improving their own lives and who make excuses for their situations instead of working hard to improve themselves are not empowering. They should not be a part of our associations. There are even those who would want to hang around to share our success but who are not willing to share our difficulties in our efforts to reach our goals.

They will have a burdensome story to tell every time and will never want to listen. We should not be a dumpster for our associates. We can understand when circumstances arise, and we are happy to offer encouragement. However, we must be able to detect the difference between the need for encouragement and being used as a dumpster by our associates. We should also refresh our life and welcome new and good associates into our lives.

It is a part of our responsibility to ourselves to expand our circle of good associates. We should be on the lookout for seminars and business functions out of our area of specialization. We should get into the habit of networking with other businesses and make ourselves open and available to new associates who have our same agenda. It is good that we get acquainted with people in public affairs who can be an asset to us, and we must also be an asset to them. It is helpful if we keep a file card with phone numbers. It is also beneficial to extend ourselves by passing out our cards to others. We must make the effort to develop a group of powerful men and women who know our value and who know our self-worth. This must be done honestly, sincerely, and for the purpose of having good associates. In this process we must be certain not to force ourselves upon people but should stand ready to welcome honest and sincere new associates.

These new associates should share our interests, and should be involved in the business world and should be motivated. Who we know and who the person knows who know us can give us great connections and great new associates. Staying ready to meet new people and presenting ourselves as friendly is vital. Life is merely what we make it out to be and what we choose to do for ourselves and for others. Therefore we can make ourselves known in a positive and good way. Partying and hanging out is not always the best way to meet associates. Limiting your gatherings and being wise in the type of associates that you choose to encounter may help you. Targeting the area of lack or abundance in our lives and attending gatherings that are business oriented, spiritual, cultural and specific to our needs or desires is a good way to get new associates. At the same time we must consider being versatile in order to meet physicians, attorneys, accountants, computer consultants, artists, educators, authors, and people in many other professions.

Support the activities of others and take the time to attend functions. We can't just limit ourselves to the few personal friends that we have and stay in a corner. On the other hand, these functions should be attended with personal style while wearing the proper attire and with the correct motives. Do not fall into the hands of a predator. Act with great caution and common sense. Also, do not do this constantly and on every weekend, but allow space and time. However, it is needful that we surround ourselves with a well-rounded and beneficial association and associates. Remember to be selective in this process; not everyone that you meet is an associate.

It's not just the number of associates that you have that matters. Sometimes having a few good associates is better than having a crowd of bad associates. In this case 'the more the merrier' does not apply. If you can only attract very few associates, it can be better than having to please too many or a lot of associates. Count your blessing in this area. Having a few people who whole-heartedly believe in you and love you is more valuable than being with a group of people who are jealous of you and who are jealous of each other. No matter how good life gets, we should keep valuable and treasure-able associates around us. We should encourage our associates to grow and to develop spiritually, mentally and socially as we grow and develop. However, at times it is needed that we free ourselves from associates who start out good but end up bad or who are detrimental to us. When we lose associates or friends it is very painful, but we must know that as long we live this will happen to us.

There are those associates who will be in our lives forever, until we die. Others will be in our lives only for a season of time. Some associates may be in our lives just for a single purpose. When that purpose is finished, they will leave. We must know the difference, we must learn when and how to let go of various associates. This must happen in order to continue our success. Your associates will need to follow the same principle. Try to make the break-up as pleasant as possible, if possible. If there is no other way, then wish your associates farewell and continue to pray for them. However, do not allow this to be so painful that it stops you from aiming high and accomplishing your goals.

You will miss your associate, but make room for someone who is just as good. Never shut down and stop yourself from advancing in life. If you must shut down, give yourself time, but let it be temporary. Who you identify and relate closely with will expose the type of person you really are and will tell people a lot about you. We tend to associate with people who are similar to us or those who are strong where we are weak. Make sure that your associates help to balance you instead of negatively influencing you.

Sometimes people want to associate with us because they view us as strong and they can lean on or rely on us for their needs or to solve their problems. However, an associate relationship must be balanced, and problematic situations should be shared on both sides of the relationship. Some women prefer male associates to female associates. They feel that men are less argumentative and less begrudging. On the other hand, some feel that women associates are more sympathetic and understanding. There is truth on both sides of this situation. In some cases it may prove to be more successful to have a balance of both male and female associates. In other cases of male associates, there may be the risk for women of violating friendship by turning it into a sexual relationship. I caution you about this type of situation. Male/female platonic relationships may do better when they remain that way. Value and respect a good associate or friend, whether it's a male or a female. Know when you have a good associate and give back and respect the relationship. Support a healthy associate or friend, sustain them and respect them.

Know Your Friends

Name the persons, by initials that will do anything to help you.

Name the persons, by initials that you would do anything to help.

Compare your lists: Are the persons who will do anything for you the same people that you would do anything to help?

List the kind of associates that are missing in your life.

When you encounter people be aware of your needs both in associates and in friends.

SHIRLEY ROSE JONES

Notes

12 STOP! No Doormat Here

Our society seems to purposely select symbolic doormats to figuratively wipe their feet on by misusing them. In some cases this happens to nice people. When an individual appears to be nice or less assertive, some people assume that they are symbolic doormats. They get ready to symbolically wipe their feet on them by treating them without the respect that they deserve. They attempt to take advantage of their kindness, their gentleness, their timidity or their mild characteristics. In many ways people do this when they are very aggressive or insensitive and they must be mindful that they are overpowering others with their strong and insensitive personality. It is important that the aggressive person be considerate and cautious not to mistreat others who are less aggressive or less assertive. The aggressive person must be careful not to impose the doormat feeling on others.

Those with an assertive personality should continue to express their strong personality but they should be aware when others become uncomfortable due to their aggressiveness. The powerful person may feel that they should not change their manner of behavior for any reason. However, the forceful person should be aware of their over-aggressiveness and should be tactful instead of being offensive.

An intellectually powerful person should be able to be aggressive, yet skillful with his power. The intellectually powerful person should be patient enough to read situations, discerning enough to see spiritually, and watchful enough to read situations accurately. A strong personality is very attractive when used towards the right person, for the right purpose, and at the right time. On the other hand, when a strong person's conduct is demoralizing to others, this conduct is not effective. When the strong person uses strength responsibly, they are able to be aggressive while respecting the less aggressive person.

A person, who is less aggressive, easily persuaded, and who is nice because they are afraid of being misjudged may want to mentally wear a 'no doormat here' sign. This is intended to alert people that niceness must not be misjudged. Wearing this mental sign means being conscious but not overly sensitive. Be conscious that some people will assume that kindness can be easily controlled, manipulated, or used for the benefit of others, while the person who is showing the kindness is hurt or is being taken advantage of emotionally, spiritually, psychologically or physically.

Wearing this mental sign means being aware when your kindness or less aggressive characteristic is disrespected, unappreciated, trampled, or misunderstood. It means having the flexibility and consciousness to know when to use a quick habitual practice of being firm, quick, but pleasant. It means learning and practicing how to use clear and precise statements, comments, and actions to send clear and precise feedback and messages. Even if you do not win or you are not the last to respond, let your final response be quick, firm and meaningful. It means making the effort not to resort to crying or whimpering. Crying, pleading and surrendering only feed into other people's power. At the same time, no verbal or physical fighting is allowed. Resorting to arguments or loud talking can lead to a verbal or a physical fight.

Learn to detect when a person is looking for a confrontation in order to make him or herself feel good or feel better. In this instance, adopt a silent method. There is an old phrase, "Silence is golden." Sometimes not saying anything at the right time, for the right purpose can be very effective. The person who is easily persuaded should be aware of which technique to use at the appropriate times to exemplify the 'no doormat here' symbol.

'No doormat here' means to become skillful in sending the message to others that they should take their frustration to the right place, but not out on you. It means that when the aggressor is not managing their problems correctly, you use the acquired and appropriate technique to make the aggressor aware that their behavior is inappropriate and that it will not be tolerated by you. It means that you have the courage and are truthful enough to imply and to say calmly and directly that you will not accept baggage, pain, negative or hurtful behavior from anyone.

Although it may feel awkward, know that you cannot allow others to misuse you, to take you for granted, or to hurt you. Some may even demand that you support them and meet their needs or may try to corner you into saying yes all of the time, even when you really want to say "no". Saying "no" when you want to say "no" is a right thing to do. There are those who are very selfish, spoiled and demanding. They have ways and methods of imposing themselves on others by insisting that the world meet their needs, no matter how shallow or selfish those needs may be.

Whenever you feel pushed and improperly approached, or when you just don't feel up to it, respond by saying no, I am not available, or I am not able. These are appropriate responses. The point is that you should not accept responsibilities from others that make you uncomfortable or that make you feel imposed upon. Be mindful that those who are unselfish and reasonable should not be offended by "no" or by any other response. Instead they should respect you, appreciate and understand your honesty. Saying no without an explanation is also a good way of making yourself clear, and it is an appropriate way of managing the selfishness and the self-centeredness of others. In order to not feel like a doormat, you must know within yourself that you deserve respect, love, and care no matter what kind of circumstances or environment you are living in. Everyone deserves the same respect and everyone has the same rights. We all must submit to this concept internally. Although an individual may have a higher status, have lots of money, be more educated or enjoy a better environment and circumstances, they still do not have the right to disrespect others.

Those who are humane and sensible will not value, treasure, or respect substances over human beings. If you are poor and even if you feel down and out, still do not allow anyone to make you feel as though they are better than you. Begin spiritually, get up, and do whatever you can about your circumstances. Do not accept the doormat feeling. Do not allow an arrogant person to push you down because just like an arrogant person can get up on a ladder, they can fall down from the same ladder. You can defend yourself by doing your best for yourself and not allowing others to take advantage of you, your circumstances, or your lack thereof.

13 THE KEY

You have within you the choice to completely open up doors to success. You also have within you the choice to completely close doors that need to be closed. When you make the decision to exercise this choice you are able to cause your circumstances to change. The most important key that you possess is the choices that you make on a daily basis or in every situation. Some people have fantasized upon the thought that there will be some kind of magic or some kind of luck that will be their key to turn their lives around. In this case they have not acknowledged the key that is within themselves. Although you will have experienced power, blessings, and miracles that will have changed your life, the choices that you make will determine whether you honor your blessings or whether you lose your blessings.

The key to any circumstance is within you, not outside of you. No one has the power to turn you on and off, in and out, opened and closed unless you give up your choice, and you let them do it by making your choices for you and utilizing your key. Your ability to accomplish your life's entire goals is not only influenced by your circumstances but guided by the choices that you make. Accomplishing your goals is also impacted by the time in your life when you make your choices.

Most mistakes can be rectified by a new, fresh or better choice. Discover your power by exercising good choices, and take note of the outcome. Continue to take control of your decisions, will power, and your choices--and watch the difference in results. Use good choice to empower your courage, your bravery and your strength in pursuit of fulfilling your purpose.

Live your life each day in a manner as if you must fulfill your purpose of the day. Continue to utilize your choice as one of the keys to refuse any negativity that others may bring you. Once you are able to act upon healthy choices you will live life more fully instead of having life living you.

Although your lifestyle may be impoverished, your choice will be one of the keys to bring you out of poverty. Nothing and no one can lock up your opportunities except your poor choices.

Some of these poor choices include the choice to do nothing about unpleasant situations and the choice to be powerless. Also, some choose to accept failures and choose to never overcome them. Some even choose to blame their unfavorable situations on everyone else but themselves. However, taking control of your choice will help to lead you into a successful and a prosperous future.

Another one of the keys to having control of your life is education. This process called education begins even before we are born. We are able to acknowledge sounds and appreciate them at this early stage. At an early age we know the difference between joyful singing and sudden crying. Knowledge is when we gain the know-how or the awareness of an event. During our school years many teachers attempted to teach us how to study and how to achieve a higher level of knowledge. Some of us felt that this experience was an imposition and we were miserable throughout our school years. On the other hand some of us excelled in school and became knowledgeable. After high school, in many instances there was no one to push us to learn. In some cases intense learning ended at this point for those who stopped at this level. Regardless of your position now you must be inspired internally to educate yourself and to be involved in educational experiences.

It is no surprise that you are better equipped for the challenges of life when you invest time, effort and money in your education. Although going to school may be difficult, life feels better and life is more promising when you are doing something positive such as learning. Also, to enhance your education you can read a fascinating book that interests you and educates you at the same time. Just as you exercise your physical body you must exercise your brain. Just as you feed your physical body, you must feed your brain with proper nourishment and with powerful ideas.

There are many ways to educate you. One way is by going to college or by taking continuing education courses. Find your point of interest and take accredited and certified courses in your interest. On the other hand, find your weakness and take courses to strengthen that weak area. For example, many women need to expand their knowledge on finance and investment in order to take control of their destiny. Step up and take the challenge and turn the lock open to financial management.

Every woman should learn to earn, to manage, and to invest her money. Women should also become more aware of finances and ways to seek tax shelters. Other means of learning include utilizing visual aids, the Internet, reading and writing, the library, and searching for other methods to enhance your knowledge. In our society, the rule implies the more you know the more you earn. In many ways, more knowledge equates to more money.

Establishing good listening skills is another key that can help to move you in the right direction. Learning to listen is also a good way to obtain more knowledge and more wisdom. Many of us take great offense at constructive criticism and turn a deaf ear. Some of us do not want to hear anything that anyone has to say. We simply refuse to listen to anybody. We make tremendously hard and harmful mistakes in this way. Sometimes we act as though we have all of the answers and that we know it all. However, it is advantageous to take the time to listen with your ear and with your heart to what a friend or family member has to say. Listen to others share their thoughts and concepts and learn from them.

Conversation and exchanging knowledge is a good way to help make good decisions if you have good listening skills. When you learn to listen you can hear and see others' mistakes and avoid these mistakes in your own life. You will hear from the elderly person and be able to bridge the gap between their generation and your generation. You will enjoy the sweetness of their experiences and find a path to build upon what they have started. You will become a part of a network and will be able to enjoy the benefits from their life experiences. Many of the elders wish that we would learn to listen to them because they have a lot to tell us and to pass on. Many of them have wisdom that we need to hear and wisdom that we need to apply to our lives.

Listen to a wise person. Observing a wise person, distinguishing the good from the bad, and choosing the good can increase your wisdom. Adapt the good mannerisms and disregard the bad ones. To gain wisdom, learn to think through your actions before performing them. Balance the benefits, and if there are consequences don't ignore them. Consider consequences because they will not disappear or go away.

Good planning is essential. Try not to be sudden, impatient or rushed in your decision-making. Instead try to be cautious, deliberate, and as exact as possible in every action. Allow these approaches to become an innate part of your behavior. In other words, don't think too much or too little, but take the time to think enough. Also, don't neglect important situations but don't give them so much time that they overwhelm you. Turning the key of wisdom in your life will help to prevent many mistakes in your life.

Another key is planting good seeds into good ground. This may be a spiritual concept, but be deliberate in doing good deeds every day. Perform your good deeds in a spiritual context. Do your good deeds to others in need such as the sick, the hungry, the homeless, the fatherless, the motherless, the brother-less, the sister-less, the friendless, and the mentally challenged. Deposit your good deeds into people who really need it and will benefit from it. This indicates that you are planting good seeds in a good ground. By no means should you waste your good, nor should you open the door to being used, but don't allow these warnings to prohibit you from applying good principles. Giving is the reciprocal of receiving. Also, know the law of farming: whatever man sows that shall he also reap. If you sow or plant corn, you can only get corn. If you sow or plant nothing, you can only get nothing. If you sow or plant goodness, you can only get back goodness.

Don't forget the most important key, which is faith. You must know God for yourself. Faith is essential in overcoming hard times. Utilize these keys and the many others persistently to reach an area of completeness and success in your life. At any given time, you can decide that you can turn the key and open doors of success in your life.

14 Ingredients For Success

Deep within our hearts, deep within our souls, and deep within our subconscious we wonder: how do they do it? We really want to know if the characteristics of successful people are different from our characteristics, or if the habits of successful people are superior to our habits. We lay aside our jealousy, and with some uncertainty, we may even wonder if successful people are special, or if successful people are just lucky. Most importantly, at times the sudden thought goes through our minds---can it happen to us like it happened to them? We surrender ourselves to these thoughts and to these considerations because it's difficult for anyone to pinpoint the path of rich people's success, the path of their money, and the path of them having it all. We also consider these thoughts and considerations because within most of us is a desire to reach a high level of success for ourselves. Within most of us there is a desire, and there is a passion to make it to the top.

This passion is deep within our culture, and this passion was evident with our parents and with our grandparents. Many of our parents and grandparents made great efforts to discover the components for success. In their efforts some of them learned many things and some of them made great accomplishments, while some of them suffered and died without reaching their goals. Therefore, the generations before us became determined to pass on to us everything that they had learned about getting to the top. In their effort, our parents and our grandparents used kind methods and sometimes they used what some considered being stern methods in this endeavor. Some of their methods include instances when some of us were spanked and some of us were denied our leisure time so that we could stay focused on the most important things for our lives. Also, in their efforts our parents and our grandparents did everything to prevent interference from getting in the way of us getting to the top. They wanted to stop the negative influences of peer pressure and they wanted to stop the negative influences of us being in the wrong crowd. They had high hopes for us.

Their high hopes started while we were their innocent and their wonderful baby in their womb. At the first sound of our heartbeat, some parents' dreams and their great anticipations of our success were already real to them. On that beautiful and blessed day when we were born into the world, some of us were greeted by our parents' dreams, anticipations and high hopes for us. For example, when some of our parents gave us the first suck of milk, and our eyes met their eyes the strong desire for our success was already present in their eyes. Some of us felt their desire as love, but we didn't as yet understand their desire. Many years later our parents' desire became our own desire and we established within ourselves the passion for success for ourselves.

Many of us became more aware of our desire for success as we grew older, and we became more involved in the struggles for success. In our struggles we encountered others with great ambitions for success and we competed with them in many ways. For many people, becoming successful is a lifetime challenge. Also, due to the severity of the great challenges for success many people have given up and they let go of their own dreams. Unfortunately for some others, the difficulties that they encountered weakened them instead of making them strong. Therefore they resorted to using drugs or alcohol to soothe the pain of the self-doubt that hindered their success. Due to these experiences and many others, it became clear to many people that becoming successful is not easy.

Despite all of these and many other uncertainties, many of us continue to look up and we continue to hope that we can keep up with those who are getting to the top. However, in spite of our hope and in spite of our determination, sometimes many people still have the concern that getting to the top may be reserved for somebody special.

The success stories of others still ring in our ears, as the media feels compelled to bombard us with the stories of those who have made it to the top. Book publishers still bombard us with self-help books and autobiographies on popular people in an effort to show us the way to the top. Yet we continue to struggle within ourselves for specific answers and for specific directions on how to achieve success. Some of us have even tried to use the pathway of those who have 'made it' as a guide to success.

We know that those who have made it to the top have a real story to tell; therefore we are compelled to read and to listen to their stories. We are moved by their experiences, and we want to identify with them through their experiences. By listening to their stories we want to feel their emotions and we want to capture their success. Deep down within us we want success to happen for us too. We want the plain truth, simplified. We want simple ingredients that we can apply to our lives daily that will help us enjoy the sweet flavor of success.

Let's acknowledge one particular seasoned ingredient that the world continuously needs. The importance of this ingredient is profound and the possession of this ingredient will make a difference in the world. This ingredient is so powerful that it will change lives and will overcome any recession in the economy. This ingredient will overcome depression and will overcome difficult times in a person's life. It is such a necessary ingredient that we must impart a dash of it to the development of our children. As we encourage our children to achieve success we must remember to give them a serving of this powerful ingredient daily. This ingredient is joy. Don't underestimate the power of joy! We must have joy and we must also have ways to remain joyful. There are many Biblical references to joy, which indicates to us that joy has been around for a long time and that joy is as old as the Bible. These Biblical references also indicate to us that joy is important and that joy needs to be maximized in our daily living no matter what betides us. For example, one reference, James 1:2 KJ Version says, "My brethren count it all joy when ye fall into divers temptations." Verse 1:3 informs us that with certain knowledge we can do this. "Knowing this, that the trying of your faith worketh patience."

Therefore, we see that joy must be maintained no matter what we are going through. We see that joy is very important if we want to overcome obstacles in our path to success. When we have joy, nothing can keep us down. With joy present, we can see clearly. We can see that our hardships are the experiences that we need so that we can join others at the top. Joy affords us not to take our hardships personally. Instead, joy expands our perspective and joy makes life look favorable to us.

Joy makes the world look favorably toward us, which makes our success seem within our reach. However, our joy must not be temporal; it must be permanent. Joy within our heart makes triumph over challenges fun, instead of triumph over challenges being a drag-down-knock-out-fight. When we adapt to rejoicing we sleep better, we are more peaceable, and we think more clearly. We also become more energetic because we don't carry life's responsibilities as weights on our shoulders.

When we have joy we can rejoice after any difficult situation. Circumstances cannot defeat us nor discourage us. Therefore, when circumstances cannot keep us down we are free to work more persistently towards achieving success. A joyful state of heart is a major ingredient for a successful life and for a healthy life. God is the source of joy. Also, we can add to our God-given joy by reading a good book, by watching a good movie, by associating with pleasant people, by utilizing humor, by being satisfied with our total self, and by appreciating life.

Faith is another ingredient that strongly influences you towards success. Faith defies the "1 can't" mentality and posts "1 can" in place of it. Faith displays "1 can" at all times so that everyone around you can be strengthened and they can enjoy the sweet flavor of your faith. Faith cannot be denied. Faith helps to lead you toward success while at the same time helping you to overcome obstacles. Faith will physically see you to the outcome of your efforts, faith will fuel your success, and faith will make you smell the sweet scent of a far distant goal. Faith shortens this distance between you and your distant goals by bringing your dreams into reality, and faith makes the impossible become possible. Faith makes your success become present. Faith confronts the things that impede you in your life as you are on your journey towards success. Faith does not back down from obstacles. Faith arms you with the spiritual weapons needed to do mental battles, and faith helps you to win every time. Faith is a necessary and a powerful ingredient for success.

On the other hand, doubt and negative competition can surround us. Also, there are many adverse situations in our environment that can make us doubt or that can make us become fearful. Still, having doubt and knowing fear are the opposite of having faith. Therefore, we must recognize doubt and fear whenever we are confronted with them. Whenever we are presented with doubt and with fear we must have words and actions of faith ready to destroy all doubts and all fears. Words such as, "all things are possible to them that believe," and "if I can believe it, I can achieve it," must be on the tip of our tongue at all times. We must act upon these words.

The instant a shadow of doubt or fear comes around us or crosses our minds, we must repeat these words out loud until we are comforted and until our faith is restored. We must have strong sources of faith ready at all times in order to restore our faith. When our faith is restored we can continue. When our faith is restored we can continue on the path for our success to the point of achieving our goals. Before getting to the point of achieving our goals we must first believe that our goals can be achieved. Although others have achieved these same goals before us, we must be confident that these goals can be achieved by us. In this live consciousness of achieving goals we then rely on faith instead of relying on luck, or we rely on faith instead of relying on chance.

The knowledge of this belief principle leads us to the action of researching and leads us to the action of gathering up resources to achieve our high level goals and success. Therefore, the sole responsibility of success is not left up to the universe. It is not even just for the gifted, nor is it just for those who are special. Success is eminent, and success is for anyone who puts faith into action. We all have the opportunity to achieve success. We need faith also, because faith counteracts hardships and stumbling blocks. Faith is strong enough to help us to stand up against what appear to be mountainous obstacles in our lives, and faith will also help us to destroy these mountains. Faith will help us sweep away these barriers and faith will smooth our pathway to success.

The ingredients of seeking and knocking are also very important. We cannot forget the old policy of seeking for opportunities and knocking on the doors of these opportunities. We must often consider the fact that so many opportunities are just waiting for a person who is willing to seek for them and someone who is bold enough to knock on the doors for these opportunities. For instance, there are foundations just waiting for a person who is seeking to find them. There are scholarships available waiting to be awarded. There are government funds and grants, in the sum of millions of dollars, waiting for someone. There are investors who offer the help that everyone or that anyone may need. There are resources that are available, there are short cuts that are available, and there are all of the solutions available that we need; all of these are there only for the person who is seeking. We must seek all resources and explore them thoroughly. Then we will know that all things are ready and are waiting for us to find them and use them for our success. However, we must become seekers. When we seek thoroughly we will find successfully. Therefore, look for what you need; everything that you need is available for you.

That which you need is in the libraries, on the Internet, on the school campus, in the banks, or they are in a book in the bookstores. All informational guides will enlighten you. These sources are only for the curious minds, and they are only for those who are determined to seek for success. A laid back attitude and a tired disposition cannot find success. We must become active and persistent seekers, which will lead us to becoming successful finders. When we have sought well and have become finders, we must possess the confident joy to knock on doors with determination. We must have the faith and the confidence to knock on the doors of success.

When we knock on the doors of opportunities we must knock with boldness. We must knock on these doors with our own unique personality and we must make our knocking recognizable. Approach those who hold our opportunities with respect, with joy, and with faith. When we possess all of these ingredients collectively, and when we knock on one door and that one door does not open the first time we are not discouraged. We are prepared to knock again, or to knock on another door. The principle stands that if you are persistent in knocking on doors of opportunities, you will wake up someone. Someone will come to the door and they will open the door. Therefore knock, knock, and knock.

Another effective ingredient is persistence. This is the ability to continue to strive for success despite repeated failures. A persistent person will not accept the response "no" as final. Instead, a persistent person will set goals and will not give up or quit until their goals are achieved. A persistent person will not procrastinate or delay. Instead, a persistent person works on a schedule and works in a timely manner to achieve goals in a timely fashion. A persistent person finds methods to reach a certain level of achievement in a particular time frame. There are no excuses for slackness or wasting valuable time.

In order to become persistent, put your short-term goals on a thirty-day calendar. Check your calendar on a daily basis to keep yourself on task. Delete distractions such as TV programs, unimportant phone calls, and other activities that waste your time. You may tape your favorite TV shows and watch them in your leisure time. You may talk to your friends after you have finished with your task instead of allowing social conversation to interrupt your work time. When one short-term goal is finished, set another one and learn to do this consistently. Allow this system of working to achieve short-term goals to become a pattern in your life, and utilize the same pattern to achieve long-term goals.

Respect is another ingredient that will take you very far. Self-respect takes precedence over other forms of respect. Those who do not respect themselves will also struggle to respect others. Respecting yourself will keep you in line and will help you to maintain good conduct. Self-respect will make you dress for success and self-respect will make you ready when success comes. Self-respect helps to keep your mind out of the gutter and it helps to direct and keep your mind in the mainstream of achieving success. Self-respect will keep your mouth speaking respectable words about others. Self-respect allows you to address your co-workers in the proper manner. This kind of self-respect leads to you respecting your human family and the total environment. Respect gives you a certain appreciation for everything and for everyone.

A respectful attitude will empower others to consider you for the things that you have requested of them. Respect makes you pleasing and it makes you appropriate. Practice this sort of conduct by speaking pleasantly to those in your environment. Hold the door for the next person who follows you. Take the time to acknowledge people, smile and show them respect in every way. Show respect to your children and other family members by saying "please" and "thank you" when necessary. Respect will take you up the ladder of success and it may even cause you to sparkle and to be remembered by the right people.

15 CONTROL YOUR MONEY EMOTIONS

Money has a direct connection to our emotions. So many times a feeling of fear, sadness, or depression is associated with how we manage our money. When we are unable to buy the things that we need also cause negative emotions. However, we experience a feeling of higher self-esteem when we show control over our money. Therefore, we must find ways of having more money to put in our pockets and to save for our security. We must take the necessary precautions to ensure that the emotions that we have towards money are healthy ones. We do this by taking control of our money instead of letting the lack of money cause us to have despair.

In the economic squeeze of today, many families work only to pay bills while many others struggle to live above the poverty level. Single parents suffer the most and many single parent households lack the funds required to meet their basic needs. In many family households, two salaries are not enough to protect the household from financial struggle. Many families feel the discouragement of losing almost 30% of the money that they work so hard to earn. For these reasons, money is one of the most important substances and we need more of it in our pockets now!

Many of us work a full forty-hour week and some of us work additional hours in overtime. We still do not enjoy a substantial amount of the money that we earn. Income gets away from us in so many ways; therefore we endure the problem of having little or no money left in our pockets. Some of us endure severe financial struggles and feel that there is no way out of these struggles. On the other hand, many people live from paycheck to paycheck and hope for a miracle to turn their finances around. Others cannot even make ends meet. These factors cause emotional pain, great hardship, and burdens.

In such an economic squeeze as we face today we must take control of our money by becoming more money wise. We cannot allow the status of the economy to lead us into more financial worries. Therefore become more money wise by taking the initiative to count your money. Counting your money helps you to know how much of your money goes to Social

Security, Federal and State Tax, health and dental benefits, and to investments such as your 401K. Take the time to count your money to be certain that you are getting compensated correctly for your hard work. Count your money to make sure that everything adds up and that all of your money is accounted for in your paycheck every time. Counting your money is also advantageous in several ways. Counting your money will identify your tax category. When you locate your tax category you will understand if working overtime places you in a higher tax bracket. If this is the case, then more of your overtime money will go into paying taxes. Therefore, assess how much overtime is needed for you to keep a higher percentage of your money instead of paying the highest percentage of your overtime money to Uncle Sam.

Counting your money gives you emotional control and it allows you to face the facts about how much money you have to begin your financial planning. Moreover, counting your money is the beginning of money management because it is impossible to manage and to keep your money if you know very little about it. Counting your money will help you determine if you need a second job and will help you determine how many hours to work on that second job in order to raise your income. Most importantly, when you count your money it may surprise you that you are bringing home more money than you had realized. It may also surprise you that you had been accomplishing so much with what you had; therefore you may be able to save a lot with just a little more money. Count your money so that you can determine how much you can save and put in your pocket.

Account for the amount of money that you pay on all bills. Never get into the habit of working and just sending off monthly payments unless you are sure that you are paying the most cost effective monthly rates possible. Investigate concerning the amount that you pay on all of your bills and seek to lower your payment. Become a detective about the money that you pay and find the financial break that is due to you. In most cases there are financial advantages that we will never know about unless we do some investigating or until we request a financial break.

Most black customers can win and can save money if we investigate because we are over-charged in many cases. For example, in some geographical areas throughout the fifty states, black customers pay twice as much as other customers for almost everything. However in some of these instances there are price deductions and price percentage breaks that we don't know about. Unless we become a detective about the money that we spend, we won't find the deductions and the price percentage breaks that are due to us.

Another way to save is to seek out the most cost effective insurance for all of your insurance policies. Use the yellow pages, ask friends about low cost insurance, and go to the library and the various websites to find the most cost effective insurance for your car, house, life and everything that you need to insure. Talk to your car insurance holder and consider paying a higher deductible and fewer monthly payments. Increase your deductible to $1,000. If you are a careful driver, and if you do not drive a lot, this may be a suitable option for you. Also, ask them if they will decrease your payments if you remain with them for a long period of time. Ask for any new discounts that are now available that were not available previously.

Most people who do their homework can usually save 30% on what they are now paying for insurance policies. Save 30% from your insurance policies and put this money into your pocket. The hard earned money of many people is wasted because they get ripped off with high insurance rates, high mortgage rates, high cell phone costs, high car notes, high interest rates, and high tax brackets every month. However, when you become a detective about cost and when you obtain the best price on these monthly bills, you can save at least 50% and you can put this money into your pocket. Be determined to find a better price than the price that you are paying right now. As you have worked hard to make your money, make the commitment to work even harder to keep your money and to put it into your pocket.

Save more money by stopping other financial waste. Discover financial waste, gather up this financial waste, and then be determined to save the money that you have gathered up. It may in some cases seem as though you are doing everything that you can do already, and you may not even see any waste, but there is a hole in your pocket somewhere. We waste money in many ways. We find ourselves spending money at snack machines for sodas and snacks, we spend money at coffee breaks, we spend money for lunch, and we eat at expensive restaurants too often. These coins and these dollars add up.

Begin to control these financial wastes by packing your lunch while you are fixing dinner or after you have eaten dinner. Buy snacks and juices in bulk packages at discount stores and bring them to work instead of spending at the vending machine. Enjoy your coffee breaks with your own choice of teas, juices or snacks that you bring from home. You can save $50.00-$100.00 from careless spending on food each month. Also, limit your restaurant habits and put your savings in your pocket.

Save money on the price you spend for self-maintenance and personal up-keep. For example, consider if your hair do is really worth the price that you pay, and consider if you could get the same styling about $10.00-$20.00 less. Consider a low maintenance style. After you have done your shopping around, let your beautician know that you have found a place that is charging you less for the same hair care and fancy hair do. Remember that there are still good beauticians who offer reasonable prices who are looking for regular clientele. Find such beauticians and salons and begin to pay a cost-effective price for your hair up-keep, your manicures, your facials, your eyebrow tweezing and for all other personal up-keep.

Another area where you can save more money is your dry cleaning bill. Consider if the cost of your dry cleaning could be decreased. Save money by not cleaning one or two garments at a time. Instead, ask for a discount price for cleaning 10-15 garments or more at a time. You can shop around and find cleaners who will give you discounts for cleaning large quantities of garments. Save money from transportation. Begin by shopping around for a gas station in your area which offers good gas and that will give you more gas for less money per gallon. Many people ignore this means of saving, but just as often as we fill up our gas tank, we can save as often as we can. Forsake the habit of just randomly stopping at any gas station to fill up your tank at any cost. Also save money by checking your oil in your car every three months or every 3,000 miles to prevent major transportation breakdowns. Be even more conscious and obey the traffic laws to prevent getting traffic and parking tickets, which develop unwanted bills.

When you use preventative measures you save yourself money that you can put into your pocket. You will be surprised at the amount of money that you will save yearly if you add up these costs. Much discipline is needed to control your shopping urges. Do comparison-shopping and use the stores with the most discounts on items that you buy. Avoid unplanned shopping and rushed shopping. Be sure to allow yourself sufficient time to compare prices and to find sale prices on items that you use.

Pay your bills on time to avoid late charges and to build up good credit. Paying bills is neither as burdensome nor as overwhelming as it is presented to be. Look at paying bills as just taking care of the responsibilities that you have accumulated due to your particular needs. Also, when you pay your bills on time you are less stressed. When you are less stressed you are less likely to do impulsive spending and create unwanted bills. Your goal is to only establish bills that you can afford to pay.

Self-discipline is needed to put yourself on a schedule and to enjoy paying your bills on the date that you have made the agreement to pay them. When you follow through with your agreement, you establish good credit and you avoid late charges on your bills. You can enjoy taking care of your responsibilities. Late charges on bills will set you back and will put a financial hole in your pocket, while paying your bills on time will keep you in a better financial position and save you money to put into your pocket.

Make an enormous effort to control bank charges. Remember that it's your money and that the bank does not have control of your money. You are the only one who has control of your own money. Therefore, make the bank a pleasant place to keep your money and to give you access to your money. You can do this by selecting a bank that accommodates your needs. Do not accept a bank adding numerous charges to your account each month. Examine your bank statements for excessive service charges and question any unwanted charges.

Many banks offer exceptional services to customers. Therefore, find a bank that will offer exceptional service without excessive service charges. A penny saved can become five pennies earned if this penny is invested. Therefore don't allow the bank to invest your pennies for themselves but be sure that you invest your own pennies for yourself, because these pennies are your money. Don't give the bank a penny. Also, avoid writing bad checks and then paying for overdraft. Instead, keep the balance in your account high so that the bank will pay you interest for holding your money instead of you paying for bounced checks. Keep the interest from the bank coming, and put your money in your pocket.

Get a money attitude! Become conscious about your money. Don't allow bills or the lack of enough money to get you down. Be in high spirits about every opportunity to save money. Look for sales with joy and always ask if there is a discount on your items. Smile about it; you may be about to save some money. Seek to get interest on your money instead of paying high interest and late charges on your money. Shop at stores where you can save money and where you can get more money per cost.

It's not how much you make but it's how much you keep from what you make that counts. Your positive attitude about this fact can change your money motivation. Your high energy about keeping your money will help put you in the position to gain more money. In this way you can save money and put it into your pocket and feel good.

16 Celebrating Womanhood Every Day

We should know that a woman enjoys great excitement and exceptional satisfaction when she realizes the power in womanhood. It takes some women forty years to reach this height of satisfaction and excitement. When this height is reached, a woman feels the power of self-ownership and self-confidence. Although the burdens of sex bias that society exercises about women are still present today, the woman who realizes her power triumphs in spite of them. When a woman knows who she is, unattainable goals become a challenge that is achievable, and it is a pleasure for her to meet them and to win. In this case, although the struggle of bringing up children with periods of sadness, exhaustion, depression, and uncertainty may still be present, the woman who understands womanhood prevails, since she does not give up.

Instead of giving up, this woman allows these obstacles to become moments of personal growth and periods of personal development. Due to her heightened consciousness, the self-confident woman no longer accepts the great pains and the many doubts that society places on being female. The self-confident woman defines herself and her eyes become open, and in her mind and in her heart she knows that women no longer have to hide or walk behind another human being. The self-confident woman knows that she can walk in front, and that a woman can lead the way. This woman and her coming out astound the world. Now it's this woman's time to achieve educational status and to direct education into power, into love, and into unimaginable success. The satisfaction and the excitement of womanhood is the full experience of this empowerment.

According to the cognitive developmental theory, gender identity is the individual's concept or knowledge that she or he is female or male. In the beginning we must teach young girls the power of womanhood so that they can also grow up to share in this kind of satisfaction and excitement. Young girls must develop great admiration for women while they are being nurtured into womanhood. It is important that young girls see themselves as smart, as strong, and as leaders during this time. They must also see themselves as remarkable and as special.

Young girls should be taught self-confidence early in life so that they can be able to overcome trials later on, and so that they do not allow these trials to spoil the excitement of being a woman. Although young girls should also be made confident in feeling feminine, looking feminine, and being feminine, young girls' confidence should also be made profound in being mentally tough. Young girls should be taught to exemplify this toughness externally when necessary and still be sexy, satisfied, and excited. In this effort to build the character of young girls they must also become comfortable in taking on any challenge that comes their way. They must also be shown how to establish the ability to endure difficulty and to overcome early in life and still be feminine.

The gender identity of being woman is a strong, supportive, and positive factor in the total personality of the female, but it is also satisfying and exciting when a woman knows her power. Everything that the woman does stems from the strength of her concept of being a woman, a mother, or a sister. Even the component of her experiences, some good and some bad, influence the woman's actions and her reactions in decisions pertinent to her well-being.

The woman with a strong concept of womanhood, motherhood, and sisterhood makes the effort to ensure that all actions and reactions in her life are very positive, although they could be motivated by the negativity of others. Actions motivated by the negativity of others include experiences that were unique to her because she is a woman such as low paying jobs, being overlooked, not being heard, not being acknowledged, and being looked at as a sex object instead of being seen as a brainpower.

All of these and many other experiences have a profound effect on every decision that the woman makes. Therefore the woman is constantly improving herself. The fact that she is a woman becomes her total personality. She never forgets that she is a woman. Also in this cosmic world, being woman is associated with a tremendous amount of anxiety. The moment that a period of relaxation is eminent in the woman's external world, someone or some situation appears which implies that the woman needs a man. In other words, people and situations try to influence the woman's inner person and attempt to make her feel that if she were a man, or if she were with a man then she would get more respect. Therefore, a state of readiness and preparedness for people's misconception or sex-biased conduct is necessary, because this kind of woman is comfortable with her womanhood.

Society often refers to this readiness and preparedness as having an attitude! In this cosmic world anxiety is always present at work, at school, at home, and just everywhere. The feeling that the woman must do everything with excellence and pave the way for other women is always present with her. The teaching that if a woman does her work excellently that her excellence will open opportunities for other women is in the woman's subconscious. Therefore the woman of power paves the way for single women, financially disadvantaged women, young women, uneducated women, and unhealthy women; she represents them all.

In moments of seclusion or privacy the self-confident woman becomes typical of her gender in many ways. She lets her anxiety get away and she enjoys girly things, such as making dollhouses and playing with teddy bears. She ventures out into sports, going to the gym, dancing, singing, cooking, and cleaning. So many things are now offered to challenge her physical being as well as her mental being. She is girl, she is girl friend, she is sister-girl, and she is friend-girl. She is full of real joy, laughter, and play. She has put anxiety behind her.

As complex as it may seem at times, the self-confident woman is capable of being the typical woman, quiet or loud, feminine and sexy; but once a person gets to know her inwardly, she becomes atypical. She works as hard as any man on any given day. This woman sets goals and she achieves them. Some of these goals that this woman achieves are very difficult, and some men could never achieve them in a lifetime.

However, in this sense the self-confident woman never competed with a man; she is just goal-oriented. The self-confident woman challenges herself as her male friends watch her, and they wonder 'who does she think she is'. The self-confident woman will try the most difficult task at times, and she will sometimes take the most difficult path. She learns how to turn her time, her knowledge, and her work into money. Nothing is taken for granted.

The self-confident woman's relationship with others reflects her attitude toward her own gender role in many ways. The self-confident woman enjoys being a woman, and she never wishes that she had been a man. This is reflected in her daily temperament. Most of her efforts are seen as empowering and helping women come out of mediocrity. The self-confident woman gives other women high aspirations. She demonstrates to other women that they can have tremendous responsibilities and still achieve their goals.

The self-confident woman's life is always successful because she doesn't see failures. This woman believes that when she falls short in a task she has learned a lot. Therefore, she does not see it as failure. She sees it as a well-learned lesson and a valuable life lesson. Therefore, the self-confident woman never has failures; she has had real life experiences and well learned lessons that made her a complete woman. She has no desire to trade her life and her experiences for any other person's. It is because of her experiences that she is who she is and she is satisfied with her experiences. The self-confident woman is a well-grounded, well-established, experienced woman who has come into the fullness of womanhood.

In her eyes there are many successes and triumphs to come, and they have already begun. When a woman realizes the power in womanhood, she has learned this valuable lesson from her life experience, which is to be a friend to herself and to allow God to 'cover her back.' She has learned the meaning of rest, peace, and taking good care of herself. She learned to support and to be supported. She has learned to give as well as to receive. No one is at liberty to 'push her buttons.' She is centered and she is well balanced. Life is paying her great rewards. No one can use or abuse her. She is a woman, and every day she celebrates.

17 WORKSHOP

Use the space below or your own notebook and write a few sentences or as many paragraphs as you like about how you feel after reading this entire book. Did this book bring you to a point of realization about your life? Are you ready to see, develop and become the best *YOU*.

WORKSHOP

These workshops are all about you. It's about finding the best of you. It's about using the best of you to find the worst of you and taking accountability to make the worst of you well. Therefore, use the space below or your notebook and make sure to list the things about yourself that you are empowered to improve. Beside each item on your list write the time frame that you give yourself to improve them. Use honesty to guide you in seeing yourself on paper. Be sure you are able to refer back to this at a later date to monitor your improvement.

WORKSHOP

After reading this book list the things about yourself that you feel empowered and satisfied about, those things that make you happy to be you. These are those things that are very easy to strengthen and that you can only improve. These are the positive characteristics that will give you the fortitude to surmount any problem. These are your strengths that you are very proud of and this book simply verifies, uplifts, and distinguishes them. Be certain that you can refer back to this at any time.

WORKSHOP

After you have made note of your strengths and your weaknesses find ways to build up your strengths. Protect your weaknesses and use your strengths to elevate your weaknesses. Make the conscious effort to work on these two simultaneously so that they will bring some balance to you. In the space provided or in your notebook list the techniques that you will utilize to use your strengths to overcome your weaknesses. Refer to other books, and tapes to find useful techniques if you need to do so.

WORKSHOP

Adjustment refers to the ways that we react to stress and the many ways that we cope with people, situations, and problems. It is most important to have documented ways that are effective to adjust to situations.

After reading this book, express your resourcefulness by concentrating on your exceptional personality. Record some effective behaviors that you can extrapolate from your unique personality that will help you to adjust to changes in your environment? List them below or in your notebook.

1.

2.

3.

4.

5.

WORKSHOP

Make a personal note about the growth that you have made already, do this by listing in the space below or in your notebook several of the unproductive conduct that you exhibited throughout your life and that you now feel ready to abandon.

1.

2.

3.

4.

5.

WORKSHOP

How strong is your commitment towards growth, development and making positive adjustments? Write a paragraph or paragraphs in the space below or in your notebook about how committed you are about abandoning the unproductive conduct that you have listed and the methods that you will use to get rid of them. Be certain that you can refer to this again.

WORKSHOP

Previously we dealt with adjustment in a defensive manner. We must have defenses ready but we must operate our lives in a proactive approach. In the space provided or in your notebook list some things that you can and will do on a daily basis to make things happen for you. For example, I will get up every morning at 6A.M. and do 100 jumping rope exercises for my cardio exercise or I will send out five e-mails every day to help my business grow. Personal growth is a journey that involves examining who we are, where we are going and what we want to become. If you get tired doing this exercise take a break but come back to this exercise and be sure to complete it slowly and thoughtfully. ***Become a professional about yourself!***

1.

2.

3.

4.

5.

WORKSHOP

Which one of these situations applies to you?

Do you overwork yourself by working outside the home then coming home to do household responsibilities?

Are you a stay at home mother who has responsibilities of the entire household?

Are you a single person with no children or husband?

Are you a single parent?

Seeing yourself on paper looks very different from seeing yourself in front of the mirror. Answering these questions make you see yourself and realize what crowds your life and should make you invent some ideas on how to un-crowd your lifestyle.

Meditate on some things that you can and will do to organize yourself and don't overwork yourself according to your lifestyle.

WORKSHOP

In the space provided or in your notebook, cleverly map out some effective methods, and effective ways that you will be able to adapt and commit to in order to relieve and un-crowd your lifestyle. Be certain that you can return to them as a reminder.

PRACTICE, PRACTICE, PRACTICE! Make your list work for you by doing everything that you put on your list. Take careful measures to know your list very well. Live the list that you ingeniously provided for un-crowding your lifestyle.

WORKSHOP

Stressors are:

Daily hassles, life events, acculturative stress, pain, frustration, conflict, type A behavior, natural and technological disasters, environmental factors such as noise, extremes of temperature, pollution and overcrowding. There are many other stressors and if you can acknowledge others that should be listed here do so by listing them below or in your notebook.

WORKSHOP

Acknowledge the immediate stressors in your life list them and resolve them. Creatively find positive ways to diminish or get rid of your daily stressors. You may acknowledge them by naming them in the space provided below or in your notebook. Allow yourself room to add to your list if you have missed some today.

WORKSHOP

One major ineffective coping strategy is catastrophizing, which is thinking that a problem or problems are so gigantic that they cannot be solved. When someone has catastrophizing thoughts they unreasonably presume that their life or life situations will be dreadful. You must believe that there are resolutions to problems, that you will utilize resources and resourcefully have a victorious outcome.

WORKSHOP

What problems do you have that you catastrophize about? Recognize those that you make really bigger than they really are and you present them as though no one has ever had problems like these before. Be sure to list them by filling them in the space below and do not catastrophize about them anymore. Find reasonable resolutions for them as you acknowledge them. Create your own worksheet if you need more space.

1.

2.

3.

4.

WORKSHOP

Are you type A personality? Type A personality is stress behavior personality.

Type A personality behaviors include:

Perfectionism, highly driven, impatient, competitive, aggressive, time urgency to the point of feeling rushed and being accident prone, reluctant to surrender control to others and share power, does everything with great speed such as eating fast, walking fast and talking fast. They overpower group discussions and dominate it from beginning to end, have heavy workload, have difficulty relaxing and are restless most of the time, and they keep themselves at a standard that no one can maintain.

Do you see how having type A personality can damage your life and your health?

WORKSHOP

Are you Type B Personality

Type B personality behavior is in contrast to the type A personality.

Type B personality behaviors include:

Having the ability to relax and pay attention to the quality of their lives instead of just accomplishments. They give themselves a sensible tempo in life to reach any goal and live life on an even pattern. In other words they do not rush through life.

WORKSHOP

How will you live your life on a more rhythmic, even and unrushed pace? Remember that adjustments are reactive and personal growth is proactive. Acknowledge ways to do this my using the space below or your notebook.

WORKSHOP

Do you have a self-regulatory system? This includes learning ways to regulate your own behavior, and ways to congratulate yourself. With self-regulation you can influence or control situations.

In what ways do you regulate your own behaviors?

1.

2.

3.

4.

5.

6.

WORKSHOP

In what ways do you congratulate yourself?

1.

2.

3.

4.

5.

6.

7.

WORKSHOP

What can you do to elevate your self-confidence? Solve this the way that you would solve a math word problem, or algebraic equation and think about it then write it out.

WORKSHOP

Would you like to go to a lady's spa, gym, or any event once or twice a year? If your answer is yes then what would you have to do to accomplish this goal. This is about relaxation and comfort so use the space provided or your notebook to acknowledge ways that you can achieve these goals.

Workshop

Some irrational beliefs are:

Disparately seeking other's approval and believing that there is no way that you can survive or become successful without the approval of people.

It is irrational to insist that everything that you do must be perfect.

Believing that life only has love and approval at all times and that you are deserving of such love and approval on a constant basis.

When you contribute success in everything that you do as meaning that you are a competent individual. If you equate success with competence at all times.

If you don't have your way and if things do not go how you want them to go then life is just terrible.

Irrational beliefs make you overly concerned about the thoughts of others and lead you to the insurmountable behavior of perfectionists. The above irrational beliefs as well as others that you may be able to acknowledge should be deleted from your life in order to discover the best you.

WORKSHOP

Acknowledge your irrational beliefs in the space below or in your notebook.

WORKSHOP

Self-efficacy expectation is your belief system that incorporates the perception that you can execute a task or live your life productively while managing stressors in your environment.

What is your self-efficacy expectation at this pivotal point in your life and relate your self-efficacy expectation to things that happened in your life. In other words what makes you think that you can accomplish your goals and live your life successfully or what makes you think that you cannot accomplish your goals and live your life successfully?

WORKSHOP

Work very hard to develop your self-efficacy expectation. Use Bible verses, affirmations, quotations from poems and books, song verses, read books that tell you that you can and will accomplish your goals, repeat these and apply them to your daily lives.

WORKSHOP

Psychological Hardiness relates to your psychic being resilient so that it buffers you against stressors. Therefore, the psychological hardened individual is dedicated to feeling in control of their lives. They are able to embark upon new challenges. There focus includes commitment, challenging, and controlling. If you had difficulty with the previous exercise which was self-efficacy expectation then focus on establishing some assertiveness and psychological hardiness.

Workshop

Would you like to name the people who distract you from making a commitment to guide your life toward positive and healthy living? You may name them in abbreviation so that only you can identify them.

What do these people do to distract you from your commitment to be happy, live healthy, and reach your destiny?

Workshop

What will you do now to get rid of excuses, and make a commitment to yourself? Fill in the space provided or use your notebook.

WORKSHOP

Unselfishly **commit to yourself** to be happy, do the necessary things that you need to do for yourself, be independent and responsible, further your education if you desire to do so, get a better job and be less stressed, confront the things that disrupt your life, reduce your stress, and psychologically, emotionally, and physically clean up your life.

Commit to yourself

WORKSHOP

Now that you are aware of what you must do to be committed to yourself are you ready to take on new challenges?

WORKSHOP

List the good, healthy and safe things in your life that you have always wanted to challenge and were afraid to do so, list them in the chronological order that you wanted to do them? Use the space below or use your notebook.

WORKSHOP

How have you prepared yourself for your new healthy, good, and beneficial challenge? Write down your preparations.

WORKSHOP

Face your challenges every day with prayer, commitment, and faith. Be confident and resourceful in finding ways to overcome challenges. Make your challenges teach you. List the challenges that have caused you pain and have left you feeling that you have failed and write down the lessons learned from these challenges. Make these challenges and lessons learned teach you.

WORKSHOP

Take control of your life and keep this control. Take control of your actions, behaviors, challenges, the negative reinforcements in your life, sources that you read and watch, and say no to negative activities and say yes to positive and productive activities. List your characteristics, situations and circumstances that you need to control.

WORKSHOP

Many times our stress can be a result of medical conditions, medications, imbalanced hormones, poor nutrition, lack of social support such as support from family and friends, lack of knowledge and information, the onset of a new disease, inability to figure out why you are feeling the way that you feel etc.

WORKSHOP

Please take the time to list the situations that you feel helpless about and acknowledge if you need medical advice for an illness or physical condition. Write down your symptoms and present them to your physician. Do not ignore them anymore. Do something about your health problem today if you have one.

WORKSHOP

Nutrition plays a role in psychological health and should not be overlooked. In many cases many people eat large portions leading to obesity, eat too late at night, and eat high fats and high carbohydrate foods. Many people do not consume the recommended vitamins, and minerals that their body need.

WORKSHOP

What negative nutritional habits do you have that you could improve? Move at a comfortable pace and don't overwhelm yourself. While you have work to do you must give yourself appropriate time to do it so that you can be effective and pleased. Come to terms with your nutritional bad habits and label them below or in your note book.

WORKSHOP

Seek the help of a nutritionist to help you eat properly and nutritionally. Seek the help of a weight trainer to help you obtain an exercise program that suits you. Also create several programs so that you can maintain and exchange them so that you will not get board.

WORKSHOP

List your favorite fruits and if you don't like any fruits learn to eat some. If you do not have any medical conditions that prevent you from eating fruits then go on a fruit exploration.

What are your favorite vegetables? If you do not like any vegetables and do not have any medical conditions that prevent you from eating vegetables then go on a vegetable exploration. Learn how to cook them nutritiously and learn how to eat and enjoy them.

What are your favorite nuts? If you are able to eat nuts without health risks go on a healthy nuts exploration. Recognize which ones agree with you physically and which taste the best. Read about these healthy foods and become quite clear on their nutritious values.

WORKSHOP

Put the healthy foods that you listed as your favorite fruits, vegetables and nuts on your grocery list weekly.

Bonus Tips For Your Self confidence

You can expand your self-evaluation by taking some of the self-assessment test that is available. Answer the questions pure and honest for this is very important. We must be able to be truthful with ourselves in order to grow to our truest potential. These tests give you some idea on areas that you can strengthen. Use your own discretion if your results satisfy you or you need a more extensive result which requires paying. Most times the results given are enough to inform you about what you can improve in your life. Do not rush to take these assessments but give yourself time to think and go deep inward to get the truth on paper. Give yourself time in between test. Take a test every few days instead of daily.

Suggested Test: Go to http://www.psychologytoday.com/tests/career

Select Career

Choose Test: Burnout, Career Motivation, Career Personality & Aptitude, Concentration, Coping Skills, Criticism, and Goal-Setting

Select Health

Choose Test: Anxiety, Attention, Happiness, Lifestyle, and Sleep Hygiene

Select IQ

Choose Test: Emotional IQ, and What Type of Smart Are You?

Select Personality

Choose Test: Assertiveness, Attention Span, Egoism/Altruism, Locus Of Control, Motivation & Needs, Optimism/Pessimism, Perfectionism Test, Procrastination Test

Select Relationships

Choose Any Test You Think You Need

Begin with these tests to help you asses yourself and branch out into your own self discovery.

YOU CAN START YOUR CREATIVITY BY BUILDING YOUR OWN WEBSITE

Here Are 6 Reasons You Need A Website

To advertise so you can make money 24/7.

Use your website to sell your products and services.

To give yourself a specialized/professional image.

It keeps your business doors open 24/7 365 days/year.

People from all over the world can see it and purchase your products.

It is your platform to provide business information.

You can change it at anytime without any cost.

Go To: http://createyourownwebsiteonline.com/

MOTIVATIONAL VIDEOS

TAKE YOUR DREAMS SERIOUSLY

http://www.youtube.com/watch?v=K4iYxniW1m0

SELF MOTIVATION

http://www.youtube.com/watch?v=fpOS8YfuFbo

REACH FOR THE STARS

http://www.youtube.com/watch?v=bQLHh860DfI

NO LIMITS

http://www.youtube.com/watch?v=z7Q3wfZwkyc

I CAN

http://www.youtube.com/watch?v=_rWA5cnAEwc

GET MOTIVATED FROM FIND YOURSELF E BOOK

http://www.youtube.com/watch?v=aVBCHxiwO0U

FIND YOURSELF

http://www.youtube.com/watch?v=6AM0yVyIqv4

TOOLS FOR SUCCESS

http://www.youtube.com/watch?v=2FTIo6rufpI

ABOUT THE AUTHOR

Shirley Rose Jones demonstrates strength of spirit and a perpetual and cognitive harmony of character. She always arises to the challenge of excellence and she is a woman of conscience. Shirley Rose Jones is the astoundingly remarkable author of this book. After many years of research on the history of the intrinsic nature of people this book arises.

Exemplary in her stance to bring forth the unknown mistruths to the all-knowing and all intelligible enlightenment, she has successfully written books for all educators, all families, and all mature ages so that history will be revealed, repented, and healed.

Gifted with the extraordinary ability to feel empathy for others, Shirley found out at an early age how to compassionately love others just as God commanded all of us to do. For this reason, she is able to help many people to live happier lives.

Shirley has made a commitment to love the unloved, to support the unsupported, to help the unprivileged, to understand the misunderstood, and to uplift the depressed through her writing and her motivational tapes and speeches.

FINAL NOTES

FINAL NOTES

SHIRLEY ROSE JONES

REVIEW